Practice for Heaven

Practice for Heaven

MUSIC FOR WORSHIP THAT LOOKS HIGHER

Gabriel C. Statom

FOREWORD BY
Ron Man

WIPF & STOCK · Eugene, Oregon

PRACTICE FOR HEAVEN
Music for Worship That Looks Higher

Wipf & Stock
An Imprint of Wipf and Stock Publishers
199 W. 8th Ave., Suite 3
Eugene, OR 97401

www.wipfandstock.com

ISBN 13: 978-1-4982-0721-8

Manufactured in the U.S.A.   02/05/2015

Contents

Foreword

"Church Music: A Functional Art." So named the late Don Hustad Chapter 2 in his *Jubilate II: Church Music in Worship and Renewal*. Far from demeaning or lessening the place or importance of church music, Hustad was seeking to elevate it by recognizing its most exalted role: serving the worship of God Almighty.

Dean Thompson concurs: "Art in the liturgical context is not an end in itself. It is instead a servant of our chief end, which is the praise and glory of God ("Art in Service of Worship" (*Reformed Liturgy and Music* 21 [Winter 1987]: 63). Thus also Mary Conway: " If 'music as art' itself is the ultimate goal, then music can even become idolatry, in which the musical art form is worshipped for its own sake, not created and presented as an offering to God or a means of praising God ("Worship Music: Maintaining Dynamic Tension," *McMaster Journal of Theology and Ministry* 7 (2006): 135–6).

Gabe Statom stands firmly in this aesthetic and theological tradition. An accomplished church musician himself, he approaches his art with the firm biblical conviction that it must point Christians to their Creator. Church music is a powerful means to an infinitely greater end: the adoration of its Giver. Properly apprehended, it "runs back up the sunbeam to the sun" (C. S. Lewis, *Letter to Malcolm: Chiefly on Prayer*, 90).

Statom points us to heaven as the proper focus and framework for our earthly worship. The glory and magnificence of God's eternal abode sets a standard, and sets a table, from which we should draw nourishment and inspiration for our church musical practices. Statom walks us through the Scriptures, as well as past and recent church history, and highlights the rich allusions to a heavenly model for our worship.

The author also advocates strongly for marshalling a wide variety of musical forces and styles for our corporate celebrations, with a special emphasis on preserving the priority, improving the quality, and broadening the repertoire of congregational song.

Statom gives sound advice for coping wisely with the realities of our present-day cultural situation, while enthusiastically calling us to "look up" for motivation, encouragement and stimulation for a church music ministry that feeds the flock, draws the unsaved, and glorifies the One who alone is worthy of our worship and of our offerings of church music.

Read and meditate on this absorbing work, and be prepared to be challenged to a more reflective and heavenly-mind planning for, leading of, and participation in corporate worship.

Ron Man, D.Min.

Worship Resources International (worr.org)
Author: *Proclamation and Praise:*
Hebrews 2:12 and the Christology of Worship
(Wipf & Stock, 2007)

Preface

FOR THOSE OF US who have been called to lead the music of the church, we are compelled to better understand the theological and biblical teachings on worship. Over the past century, there have been many wonderful contributions to the topics of worship, music, culture, and the church. This book is in no way intended to be a comprehensive history or exposition on any form of worship or music, or even of the complete biblical teachings on worship. It does serve as an impetus in forming a philosophy of music for the church that reflects her long history with a modern cultural implication based on the past but certainly looking to the future: heaven.

Because the music of the church has experienced vast acclaim and dispute these past years, the matter has become greater an issue for some than others. I want to point out that while the important matters of salvation in Christ, living in peace, caring for our world, and obeying the law of the Word, are of may seem of far greater weight than the various topics presented in this book, we should consider the eternal goals of our worship while on earth. While the type of music we present in the church is not of grave consequence in comparison to the array of pain, suffering, conflict, and turmoil in our world, the power of music can bring much calm and focus to our earthly living. My objective is to challenge the church to grasp the grand and transformational power of music in worship and to remind it of the eternal narrative we are living out here on earth. For those who have been gifted and called to this "grand feast" called worship, it is a matter to be taken seriously. Just as we expect the skill of the surgeon or engineer to be honed to perfection, so we, too, in leadership of music in the church take seriously the gift and the call.

It is my hope that as we look through the biblical and historical roles of worship, we will realize the great importance that God himself has placed on the grand worship of his holy being, and how music and singing play a vital part in this heavenly worship portrayed here on earth. My personal journey of spiritual and musical growth, as well as deep searching for the ultimate purpose of our music making on earth, has helped me to focus and formulate a philosophy that keeps me grounded in choosing music for the church service that reflects the principles and values I attempt to bring out from a heavenly point of view.

Because my area of expertise is as an organist and choral conductor, I have consequently served in historic churches with strong roots of music with choirs and organs. I have also worked in developing and currently direct music for a non-traditional service and lead the band from the piano. I have enjoyed developing a liturgical service with modern hymns and music; utilizing a variety of instrumentation; mixing folk with hymnody, blues and Dixieland; and using a variety of mix with choir, oboe, mandolin, flute, violin, penny whistle, full orchestra, string orchestra, and the like. I tell you this because I hope it will indicate that my experience is broad and I am not pushing any agenda of musical preference. I am raising questions that I ponder daily in the honor I have of selecting and preparing music for the church. My goal is to enlighten and ask questions about our thinking towards a music philosophy in the church that fully understands the implications of what we do and how we worship God on earth as a time of practice for heaven—rehearsing for our heavenly home.

Aspiring to Heaven

Unseal our lips to sing Thy praise,
Our souls to Thee in worship raise,
Make strong our faith, increase our light
That we may know Thy name aright.
Till we with saints in glad accord
Sing: "Holy, holy is the Lord!"
And in the light of heav'n above
Shall see Thy face and know Thy love.

FROM THE HYMN "LORD JESUS CHRIST, BE PRESENT NOW"
BY WILHELM IV OF SACHSEN-WEIMAR
TRANSLATED BY KATHERINE WINKWORTH

DO YOU WONDER WHAT our worship will be like in heaven? The center of our faith is based on believing in Jesus Christ, with the assurance that we will live with him and the Father for eternity. God does give us a glimpse of what that will be like in heaven. Throughout the Bible we see the pomp and circumstance that surrounds the throne of God. With angels and trumpets, white robes and crowns, we see that God is enthroned with true worship from beings that desire to give him their undivided worship and praise. The book of Revelation is filled with the kind of high praise that God has designed for his people to enter into.

The visions of heavenly worship presented throughout Scripture are the most concrete images that the Bible gives the church for interpreting how we should conduct earthly worship in our corporate gatherings. While the church universal has been clamoring to identify the best methods in presenting corporate worship over the past several decades, the issues of biblical relevance to worship are becoming more poignant as we wander far from historic practices. Church musicians, in particular, are seeking answers of how to serve God faithfully while trying to balance the demands of church leaders being influenced by growing trends of popular culture that ultimately are focused on worldly entrapments.

This book looks at the role of music in the Bible, the corporate consensus of what has been acceptable for public worship in the past, and why church music should look to heaven for creating music to aid the church's ongoing worship. The argument that God deserves our best is just a small piece of how our time on earth should be shaped by our heavenward music-making. The responsibility the church has to use the gift of music to point our earthly worship toward heaven is a rich blessing. A church that understands that music can transport the soul will reap the benefit. If our music in corporate worship imitates the descriptions of heavenly worship, we are essentially *rehearsing* for that heavenly worship. Just as a musician practices his or her instrument, likewise all our worship, and all our music in corporate worship are essentially *practice for heaven*.

A philosophy of music in the church that is biblically, historically, and musically grounded with an eye toward heaven can easily answer questions about the intent of our corporate worship music. To think of each worship service as practice for being in the presence of almighty God in the midst of his high and mighty throne will transform the mindset of the church musician. The issues of style, quality, content, and intent are less obtrusive if we look to heavenly worship to guide our decisions, selections, and approach to presenting music in the corporate church. If we view the church's corporate music as a royal gathering, our music will transcend the heavens and our time of practicing on earth will be all the greater.

The premise of this book is to help musicians develop a philosophy of church music that is grounded in biblical and theological understanding that suggests the role of music in corporate worship should transport the worshipper to the heavenly throne of our God. The purpose is to engage church musicians and pastors in evaluating current practice and to consider how music and worship should transport us to heaven.

The philosophy is one that suggests church music should be unique to the evangelical church. As we examine the implications and beauty of exploring music for the glory of God among his people, I pray that all our music until that glorious day will be a wonderful time of *practice for heaven*.

Aim at heaven and you will get earth thrown in.

Aim at earth and you get neither.

—C. S. LEWIS[1]

1. Lewis, *Mere Christianity*, 134.

PART 1

What We Know about Corporate Church Music: A Vision of Heaven

I will show you a more excellent way.

—1 CORINTHIANS 12:31B

Jesus said that our worship must be in spirit and in truth.[1] The Bible is our sole authority on what is truth, particularly when it comes to worship. The Scriptures teach us the basis of our worship, the form of our worship, and the acts of our worship. There are also instructions for the music of the church that are both explicit and implicit. Scripture is filled with illustrations of how God's children have consistently been stirred by God's presence in worship, especially through the role of music. We see references in both the Old and New Testaments where worship music has aided the corporate expression.

Likewise, there is much to learn from the historic liturgies and practices of the early church—to see how they have shaped and reformed the current practices of church worship and music. Much of what we continue today has been practiced for centuries and passed down from generation to generation. Further, a brief look at the worship practices of the present will demonstrate the diversity of ideas of what is acceptable for the church. Also addressed will be the philosophies of those serving the principles that

---

1. John 4:24.

are far from a heavenly minded approach to worship—ones that look to the world to determine how best to aid corporate worship with music.

In their introduction to *With Reverence and Awe: Reclaiming Reformed Worship*, D. G. Hart and John Muether state the importance for church leaders to connect worship practice with theology:

> . . . worship inevitably follows from theological conviction. As the apostle Paul wrote to Titus, certain things are "fitting for sound doctrine," matters such as temperateness, dignity, sensibleness, faith, love, and perseverance.[2] So too we believe that good theology must produce good worship, corporate acts of praise and devotion that fit the sound theology of the reformed tradition. On the other hand, defective theology yields inferior or inappropriate forms of worship. The Protestant Reformers understood this. The confessions of the sixteenth and seventeenth centuries were all aimed at reforming the worship of the church. For example, the Westminster divines did not merely write a confession and catechisms, but started with the Directory for the Public Worship of God before completing the Westminster Standards. Because of the close connection between good theology and appropriate worship, corporate acts of praise and devotion that conflict with Reformed theology must flow from unsound doctrine. In effect, our worship provides a barometer of our theology.[3]

We can see throughout our modern era that our church music practices have been changed dramatically, possibly because of our lack of a full understanding of how great God is as prescribed in Holy Scripture, and, perhaps, the disconnect between theology and worship practice. Instead of looking to Scripture for specific instructions on how to present worship to God, much of the music for worship now lacks the depth to portray our majestic God. We have lost the imagery of his kingship over all, and our music, which therefore affects our basic theology, has at times reduced the Trinity of Father, Son, and Holy Spirit to *dad, friend, and our feelings*. Some modern music has done a disservice to the full gospel message by deemphasizing the majesty of God and romanticizing the great sacrifice of Christ.

A church music philosophy of embracing the full gospel understanding of "who God is" will determine what music we think appropriate for the worship of him. If we hold the bar higher for God's worship than we do anything else, I believe we will see a change in how Christians view

2. Titus 2:1–2.

3. Hart and Muether, *With Reverence and Awe*, 13.

our praise of him, especially in matters of music. Our worldly traditions of creating art and music for every sort of occasion should be completely trumped by the occasion of worship. When we look to Scripture to determine the awesome and mighty attributes of our God, our earthly worship will ultimately be the practice for what we view our heavenly worship to be.

Human Perception of Heaven

Before looking at the long historical documentation that has focused on earthly worship being a grand rehearsal for heaven, we must establish the almost universal notion about the human perception of heaven. Those who believe in heaven's existence believe it to be a place much better than this earth—a place where we will experience no pain or suffering—as Scripture has taught us. It is a place where the streets are made of gold and milk and honey are flowing in the rivers. Even beyond what we learn biblically about heaven, history has always imagined heaven as a place far different from earth: more reverent, more grandiose, more peaceful, more vast, more perfect than any place we have ever imagined or experienced. C. S. Lewis says,

> Hope is one of the Theological Virtues. This means that a continual looking forward to the eternal world is not (as some moderns think) a form of escapism or wishful thinking, but one of the things a Christian is meant to do. It does not mean that we are to leave the present world as it is. If you read history you will find that the Christians who did the most for the present world were just those who thought most of the next.[4]

God has called each to this present world "to glorify Him and enjoy Him forever."[5] Forever is just that—forever—not just the time we spend on earth. The object of our earthly worship is eternal and, as Lewis reminds us, it is our meaningful purpose as Christians to look towards heaven. Certainly our time of corporate worship as the church, the music that is offered, and the sentiment of its message allow for earthly preparation for heaven—essentially practicing for heaven.

Music is certainly a part of our perception of heaven. The English poet Walter Savage Landor was known for saying that "music is God's gift to man, the only art of Heaven given to earth, the only art of earth we take

---

4. Lewis, *Mere Christianity*, 134.
5. Westminster Shorter Catechism, Q.1.

to Heaven." The importance of music and heaven are inseparable. Lewis goes on to say that,

> There is no need to be worried by facetious people who try to make the Christian hope of 'Heaven' ridiculous by saying they do not want 'to spend eternity playing harps'. The answer to such people is that if they cannot understand books written for grown-ups, they should not talk about them. All the scriptural imagery (harps, crowns, gold, etc.) is, of course, a merely symbolic attempt to express the inexpressible. Musical instruments are mentioned because for many people (not all) music is the thing known in the present life which most strongly suggests ecstasy and infinity.[6]

6. Lewis, *Mere Christianity*, 137.

CHAPTER 1

Old Testament

THE OLD TESTAMENT TELLS us much about the high regard for worship. The large scale of the resources, human and otherwise, for worship, along with the detailed instructions given indicates that Jewish Old Testament worship was a cultural priority. The Old Testament leaders took seriously the role of worship. We see many examples that have implications for us on earth trying to understand the realm of heavenly worship.

The first songs of the Bible are the Songs of Miriam,[1] Moses,[2] and Hannah.[3] Musicologists who study what music might have been like during this time point out an interesting development in the change of formality from the time of the Moses to the time of Solomon. In *The Story of Christian Music* the author states, "after the building of the temple of Solomon (about 900 BC), the liturgy becomes sumptuous and spectacular."[4] We should note that the shape of worship, its liturgy and music, were dramatically transformed with the building of the temple. This earliest biblical illustration of corporate worship indicates a distinct notion from the worshippers that a gathering of such proportion deems greater detail than their previous style of "home" worship may have garnered.

In 1 Chronicles 23:1–5, we see that King David spared no expense in securing the tools and human resources for praise.

1. Exod 15:21.
2. Exod 15:1–5; Deut 32:1–43.
3. 1 Sam 2:1–11.
4. Dickson, *The Story of Christian Music*, 1.

> When David was old and full of days, he made Solomon his son
> king over Israel. David assembled all the leaders of Israel and the
> priests and the Levites. The Levites, thirty years old and upward,
> were numbered, and the total was 38,000 men. "Twenty-four
> thousand of these," David said, "shall have charge of the work in
> the house of the Lord, 6,000 shall be officers and judges, 4,000
> gatekeepers, and 4,000 shall offer praises to the Lord with the in-
> struments that I have made for praise."

The number of people here is simply a massive representation of God's
children gathered together for worship. Our modern culture can hardly
fathom the type of events that would involve this number of people. We
think of events like the Super Bowl or a protest involving 50,000 people
when paralleling to our modern culture. And surprisingly, scholars specu-
late that the world's population at that time was a quarter of what it is now.
Can you imagine that many Christians gathering now on that type of scale?
This is a beautiful picture of how grand worship can be.

Likewise, in 1 Chronicles 25, we get an example of the musical scale of
the worship. As in chapter 23 with the reference to 4,000 instrumentalists
gathered to aid the worship, chapter 25 references the use of 288 skilled
singers.

> David and the chiefs of the service also set apart for the service the
> sons of Asaph, and of Heman, and of Jeduthun, who prophesied
> with lyres, with harps, and with cymbals. The list of those who did
> the work and of their duties was: Of the sons of Asaph: Zaccur,
> Joseph, Nethaniah, and Asharelah, sons of Asaph, under the direc-
> tion of Asaph, who prophesied under the direction of the king. Of
> Jeduthun, the sons of Jeduthun: Gedaliah, Zeri, Jeshaiah, Shimei,
> Hashabiah, and Mattithiah, six, under the direction of their fa-
> ther Jeduthun, who prophesied with the lyre in thanksgiving and
> praise to the Lord. Of Heman, the sons of Heman: Bukkiah, Mat-
> taniah, Uzziel, Shebuel and Jerimoth, Hananiah, Hanani, Eliathah,
> Giddalti, and Romamti-ezer, Joshbekashah, Mallothi, Hothir,
> Mahazioth. All these were the sons of Heman the king's seer, ac-
> cording to the promise of God to exalt him, for God had given
> Heman fourteen sons and three daughters. They were all under
> the direction of their father in the music in the house of the LORD
> with cymbals, harps, and lyres for the service of the house of God.
> Asaph, Jeduthun, and Heman were under the order of the king.

The number of them along with their brothers, who were trained
in singing to the LORD, all who were skillful, was 288.[5]

Many scholars and modern church practitioners often use these verses
to justify the importance of professional or hired musicians in the church.
While this passage does imply the importance of the role for professional
church musicians, it speaks of such a grand scale that it may be mistakenly
dismissed as inapplicable because of the scale and think "this doesn't apply
to me," "we could never do anything like that," or "my church is not that
big." Second Chronicles 7 continues to display the importance of offering
grand praise unto God:

> Then the king and all the people offered sacrifice before the Lord.
> King Solomon offered as a sacrifice 22,000 oxen and 120,000
> sheep. So the king and all the people dedicated the house of God.
> The priests stood at their posts; the Levites also, with the instru-
> ments for music to the Lord that King David had made for giving
> thanks to the Lord—for his steadfast love endures forever—when-
> ever David offered praises by their ministry; opposite them the
> priests sounded trumpets, and all Israel stood.[6]

This Scripture paints a wonderful picture of how dynamic and unique
corporate worship will be in heaven and how humanity can take the lead
in creating a dynamic worship that demonstrates the vastness of our resources here on earth. The use of trumpets, for example, were to proclaim
and respond to the praises offered up, and the singing was accompanied by
harps and stringed instruments. The grandeur and majesty expressed with
trumpets and cymbals is contrasted with the more tender sounds of harps
and lyres. Likewise, the use of instruments and the role music plays in "calling" people to worship and, in the case of Daniel, to the posture of worship
acceptable in Jewish worship.

"Now if you are ready when you hear the sound of the horn, pipe,
lyre, trigon, harp, bagpipe, and every kind of music, to fall down and worship the image that I have made, well and good. But if you do not worship,
you shall immediately be cast into a burning fiery furnace. And who is the
god who will deliver you out of my hands?"[7] Here we see the role of music in a practical function of gathering people for worship. The sound of

5. 1 Chron 25:1–7.

6. 2 Chron 7:4–6.

7. Dan 3:15.

music is used as a symbol here to distinguish the worshippers—similar to heavenward calls made in the New Testament—"the trumpet shall sound." Likewise, in the Old Testament, we see the use of musicians on a grand scale, mimicking the heavenly worship to celebrate special occasions. For example, in Nehemiah 7, for the celebration of completing and opening Jerusalem's wall, many singers were employed:

> Now when the wall had been built and I had set up the doors, and the gatekeepers, the singers, and the Levites had been appointed, I gave my brother Hanani and Hananiah the governor of the castle charge over Jerusalem, for he was a more faithful and God-fearing man than many. The whole assembly together was 42,360, besides their male and female servants, of whom there were 7,337. And they had 245 singers, male and female. Their horses were 736, their mules 245, their camels 435, and their donkeys 6,720.

One of the most profound images of worship inspired by the heavens is that of the prophet Isaiah's dream that is revealed in Isaiah 6:

> In the year that King Uzziah died I saw the Lord sitting upon a throne, high and lifted up; and the train of his robe filled the temple. Above him stood the seraphim. Each had six wings: with two he covered his face, and with two he covered his feet, and with two he flew. And one called to another and said: "Holy, holy, holy is the Lord of hosts; the whole earth is full of his glory!" And the foundations of the thresholds shook at the voice of him who called, and the house was filled with smoke. And I said: "Woe is me! For I am lost; for I am a man of unclean lips, and I dwell in the midst of a people of unclean lips; for my eyes have seen the King, the Lord of hosts!" Then one of the seraphim flew to me, having in his hand a burning coal that he had taken with tongs from the altar. And he touched my mouth and said: "Behold, this has touched your lips; your guilt is taken away, and your sin atoned for." And I heard the voice of the Lord saying, "Whom *shall I send, and who will go for us?" Then I said, "Here I am! Send me." And he said, "Go, and say to this people: 'Keep on hearing, but do not understand; keep on seeing, but do not perceive.'"*[8]

This passage paints a picture of heavenly worship that includes the angels singing in antiphon, "holy, holy, holy," as well as the image of the Lord sitting on his throne with a majestic train to his robe. The drama of God's presence is accentuated with the sound of his voice, the threshold

8. Isa 6:11–1.

shaking, and smoke filling the temple. These are all images associated with extreme grandeur. Our natural response to great things and people involve these types of surroundings. For example, in the classic film, *The Wizard of Oz*, the external surroundings of the great Oz are similar to Isaiah's vision of our Lord sitting on his throne—smoke, the loud voice, and the grand thunder. It is clear in both of these illustrations that our natural, human ideal of great power is enthroned with these sorts of majestic appearances.

The Psalms

Finally, when we examine the psalms, we see a consistent thread of worship and music pointing to heaven. Both psalms of praise and the royal psalms display the type of worship that is regal in form. The imagery of God's royal position is used throughout Scripture to illustrate His kingship:

> O Lord, in your strength the king rejoices, and in your salvation how greatly he exults! You have given him his heart's desire and have not withheld the request of his lips. For you meet him with rich blessings; you set a crown of fine gold upon his head.[9]

> O Lord, our Lord, how majestic is your name in all the earth! You have set your glory above the heavens. Out of the mouth of babies and infants, you have established strength because of your foes, to still the enemy and the avenger. When I look at your heavens, the work of your fingers, the moon and the stars, which you have set in place, what is man that you are mindful of him, and the son of man that you care for him? Yet you have made him a little lower than the heavenly beings and crowned him with glory and honor. You have given him dominion over the works of your hands; you have put all things under his feet, all sheep and oxen, and also the beasts of the field, the birds of the heavens, and the fish of the sea, whatever passes along the paths of the seas. O Lord, our Lord, how majestic is your name in all the earth![10]

"How majestic is your name, O Lord!" What a powerful statement from the mouths of worshippers. Do we really believe fully in His majesty? Do we really understand majesty in the most basic way? Allen P. Ross challenges us on how to better think of God's majesty:

9. Ps 21.

10. Ps 8.

To lift up our hearts to that transcendent glory for even a moment will have a definite impact on the way we worship. If we even begin to comprehend the risen Christ in all his glory, or faintly hear the heavenly choirs that surround the throne with their anthems of praise or imagine what life in the presence of the Lord will be like, then we can never again be satisfied with worship as usual. We will always be striving to make our worship fit for glory.[11]

Likewise, Brother Lawrence in the classic, *The Practice of the Presence of God*, reminds us that to experience God's presence in a conversational way, we must hold His majesty before us ". . . we should establish ourselves in a sense of God's presence by continually conversing with Him . . . we should feel and nourish our souls with high notions of God; which would yield us great joy in being devoted to Him."[12]In both Psalms 8 and 19, the majesty of God is proclaimed through his creation and his created beings.

The heavens declare the glory of God, and the sky above proclaims his handiwork. Day to day pours out speech, and night to night reveals knowledge. There is no speech, nor are there words, whose voice is not heard. Their voice goes out through all the earth, and their words to the end of the world. In them he has set a tent for the sun, which comes out like a bridegroom leaving his chamber, and, like a strong man, runs its course with joy. Its rising is from the end of the heavens, and its circuit to the end of them, and there is nothing hidden from its heat.

Presbyterians and Reformed congregations, in particular, have embraced the idea of praising and worshipping with a sense of majesty. Hughes Oliphant Old makes his last point in his important contribution *Worship: Reformed According to Scripture,* that,

The greatest single contribution that the Reformed liturgical heritage can make to contemporary American Protestantism is its sense of the majesty and sovereignty of God, its sense of reverence and simple dignity, its conviction that worship must above all serve the praise of God.[13]

11. Ross, *Recalling the Hope of Glory*, 473–74.

12. Brother Lawrence, *Practice of the Presence of God*, 43.

13. Old, *Worship*, 176.

Old Testament Summary

Andrew Hill has done the most exhaustive work on Old Testament worship, and his summary of music in the Old Testament is very helpful:

- Jubal is called the first of all musicians (Gen 4:21).

- Music was a part of family gatherings and celebrations (Gen 31:27; Luke 15:25).

- Music accompanied the labor of harvesting and well-digging (Isa 16:10; Jer 48:33; Num 21:17).

- Dancing was often part of musical merrymaking (Exod 15:20; 32:19; Judg 11:34; 21:21; 1 Sam 18:6; 21:11; 29:5; 30:16).

- Music was a part of worship and the temple ministry (1 Chr 15:16; 23:5; 25:6–7; 2 Chr 5:11–14; Ezra 2:65, Neh 12:27–43).

- Music was part of the court life of the kings (1 Sam 16:14–23; 2 Sam 19:35; Eccl 2:8); and also a part of the enthronement celebrations (1 Kgs 1:39–40; 2 Kgs 11:14; 2 Chr 13–14).

- Music was associated with feasting and merrymaking (Isa 5:12; 24:8; Matt 14:6).

- Music expresses a wide range of human feelings (book of Psalms).

- Music was a vital part of mourning and lament (2 Sam 1:17–18; 2 Chr 35:25; Matt 9:23).

- Music was used for the restoration of prophetic gifts (2 Kgs 3:15); and to soothe troubled individuals (1 Sam 16:14–23).

- Amos condemned idle music and feasting (Amos 6:5–6).

- Singing and rejoicing are characteristic of the righteous man (Prov 29:6).

- Music will be a part of the new covenant (Jer 31:7–13).[14]

It is clear that Old Testament temple music was a grand feast for the senses. The transcendence and awesome power of God were communicated through the worship of these people of the Old Testament. The music was a part of court and temple life and even the psalmists and prophets imagined worship in heaven to be far greater than anything that we have

---

14. Hill, *Enter His Courts With Praise*, 289.

experienced on earth. The music of the time was based on great celebrations of feasts, dedications, and family life. The role music played in the ceremonious rituals throughout the Old Testament is monumental in both content and presentation.

CHAPTER 2

New Testament

For the trumpet will sound, and the dead will be raised imperishable,
and we shall be changed. For this perishable body must put on the
imperishable, and this mortal body must put on immortality.

—1 CORINTHIANS 15:52–53

IF YOU HAVE NEVER heard Handel's setting of this text from *Messiah*, you must. You will never view this text in the same way again. This is a basic example of the power of music in proclaiming Scripture, but also sentiments of heavenly worship. Just as this wonderful passage in 1 Corinthians 15 paints the picture of the heavenly transformation, so does any music we might present in worship for his glory.

> Just as we have borne the image of the man of dust, we shall also bear the image of the man of heaven. I tell you this, brothers: flesh and blood cannot inherit the kingdom of God, nor does the perishable inherit the imperishable. Behold! I tell you a mystery. We shall not all sleep, but we shall all be changed, in a moment, in the twinkling of an eye, at the last trumpet. For the trumpet will sound, and the dead will be raised imperishable, and we shall be changed. For this perishable body must put on the imperishable, and this mortal body must put on immortality.[1]

One of the most common scriptures associated with New Testament worship is Romans 12:1–2:

1. 1 Cor 15:49–53.

> I appeal to you therefore, brothers, by the mercies of God, to present your bodies as a living sacrifice, holy and acceptable to God, which is your spiritual worship. Do not be conformed to this world, but be transformed by the renewal of your mind, that by testing you may discern what is the will of God, what is good and acceptable and perfect.[2]

Two points that instruct Christians in being a living sacrifice involve worship that is modeled by the perfected idea of heavenly worship. The instruction to present our bodies *holy and acceptable to God*, is the perfected promise that we will live out in eternity, perfected in his image. Matthew Henry, in his commentary says,

> The apostle having closed the part of his epistle wherein he argues and proves various doctrines which are practically applied, here urges important duties from gospel principles. He entreated the Romans, as his brethren in Christ, by the mercies of God, to present their bodies as a living sacrifice to Him. This is a powerful appeal. We receive from the Lord every day the fruits of his mercy. Let us render ourselves; all we are, all we have, all we can do: and after all, what return is it for such very rich receivings? It is acceptable to God: a reasonable service, which we are able and ready to give a reason for, and which we understand. Conversion and sanctification are the renewing of the mind; a change, not of the substance, but of the qualities of the soul.[3]

Secondly, Paul warns us to *not be conformed to the world*. Matthew Henry goes on to say that,

> The progress of sanctification, dying to sin more and more, and living to righteousness more and more, is the carrying on this renewing work, till it is perfected in glory. The great enemy to this renewal is, conformity to this world. Take heed of forming plans for happiness, as though it lay in the things of this world, which soon pass away. Do not fall in with the customs of those who walk in the lusts of the flesh, and mind earthly things. The work of the Holy Ghost first begins in the understanding, and is carried on to the will, affections, and conversation, till there is a change of the whole man into the likeness of God, in knowledge, righteousness, and true holiness. Thus, to be godly, is to give up ourselves to God.[4]

2. Rom 12:1, 2.

3. Henry, *Matthew Henry's Commentary*, 1784.

4. Ibid., 1785.

The implications for modern practice, especially pertaining to worship and music, will be touched upon later, but the task for church musicians and other church leaders is to be clear in communicating that the Christian life is lived differently from that of the world. Our witness is in how we live and testify to the world that we are changed. One of the most unique qualities that Christians communicate to the rest of the world is how we worship. The music and other aspects of our liturgies should highlight the discipline of Christian living expressed in Scripture, not the traditions of the secular culture, or as Paul says, *conformity to the world.*

Next, we look at the book of Hebrews to read the epistle given to encourage the church by preaching a Christ-centered reminder to run the race and to not grow weary in our journey. The Apostle Paul speaks of the kingdom of God, and we see the allusions to the heavenly throne where "innumerable angels" are in "festal gathering."

> For you have not come to what may be touched, a blazing fire and darkness and gloom and a tempest and the sound of a trumpet and a voice whose words made the hearers beg that no further messages be spoken to them. For they could not endure the order that was given, "If even a beast touches the mountain, it shall be stoned." Indeed, so terrifying was the sight that Moses said, "I tremble with fear." But you have come to Mount Zion and to the city of the living God, the heavenly Jerusalem, and to innumerable angels in festal gathering, and to the assembly of the firstborn who are enrolled in heaven, and to God, the judge of all, and to the spirits of the righteous made perfect, and to Jesus, the mediator of a new covenant, and to the sprinkled blood that speaks a better word than the blood of Abel.[5]

Here again we can liken the attitude of worship in heaven to how we can better aspire to this vision put forth while on earth—the inspiration that should challenge church musicians to this same "festal gathering" with "innumerable angels" in our choirs and music-making—but most importantly with "reverence and awe."[6]

> Finally, my brothers, rejoice in the Lord. To write the same things to you is no trouble to me and is safe for you. Look out for the dogs, look out for the evildoers, look out for those who mutilate

---

5. Heb 12:18–24.
6. See chapter 12.

the flesh. For we are the circumcision, who worship by the Spirit of
God and glory in Christ Jesus and put no confidence in the flesh.[7]

Though little reference is directly instructive to the church musician
in the New Testament, there are many references from these teachings that
we will look at in later chapters. Certainly, the instructions for Christian
love carried down from the apostles and disciples are the hallmark of life in
Christ. If we separate the characteristics of transformed living from those
of what we communicate in our corporate worship, the power of our corporate testimony will have consequences in the life of the Christian family,
community, and our churches.

7. Phil 3:1–4.

CHAPTER 3

Historical Worship

WE HAVE SEEN THAT the Bible is explicit in how we offer our praise to God through the gifts he has bestowed on us. Likewise, the post-Bible historical record lies mostly in personal or historical accounts of the church. Most of our practices have been passed down from generation to generation, with little to moderate adjustments made every century or two.[1] Our understanding of what is expected in worship and music is contained more in the oral tradition rather than in recorded documents, creeds, and prayers. We will see in this section, however, that there are implications made for the church musician as to how music in worship should be carried out. The few historic sources referenced in this chapter point us to heavenly worship and the imagery of our eternal praise of God. The very character of God's holiness and his heavenly reign have helped shape the broader understanding of how church leaders have carried out corporate worship. Some implications for the church musician can be taken from these historic standards.

This section is presented as a progression of prayer, affirmation, and instruction, concluding with the teaching from John Calvin. We will explore the various aspects of history that pertain to most of our evangelical American roots, and most uniquely to the Presbyterian perspective. While there are many great books on the histories of the progression of church music, this section serves to highlight some of the more important writings, mostly from the Reformation era, that direct and govern the church to this day. Some will be reminders; some will be new. But they will all serve

---

1. See "Summary of Church Music in the Last 2,000 Years" later in this chapter.

as a reference for us in church leadership roles as a concise overview of the relation between music, history, and heaven.

Valley of Vision: Puritan Prayers

This collection of Puritan prayers has given us a glimpse into puritanical sentiments, as well as theology. The vivid imagery, rich poetic structure, and transparent confessions of these prayers display a view of heaven from a perspective of history that is focused on devout Christian living and simplicity. These prayers can focus the attitude of any church leader, but especially the church musician, toward heavenward aspirations.

> O Lord,
>
> I live here as a fish in a vessel of water,
> only enough to keep me alive,
> but in heaven I shall swim in the ocean.
>
> Here I have a little air in me to keep me breathing,
> but there I shall have sweet and fresh gales;
>
> Here I have a beam of sun to lighten my darkness,
> a warm ray to keep me from freezing;
> yonder I shall live in light and warmth for ever.
>
> My natural desires are corrupt and misguided,
> and it is thy mercy to destroy them;
>
> My spiritual longings are of thy planting,
> and thou wilt water and increase them;
>
> Quicken my hunger and thirst after
> the realm above.
>
> Here I can have the world,
> there I shall have thee in Christ;
>
> Here is a life of longing and prayer,
> there is assurance without suspicion,
> asking without refusal;
>
> Here are gross comforts, more burden
> than benefit,
> there is joy without sorrow,
> comfort without suffering,
> love without inconstancy,

rest without weariness.

Give me to know that heaven is all love,
where the eye affects the heart,
and the continual viewing of thy beauty
keeps the soul in continual transports
of delight.

Give me to know that heaven is all peace,
where error, pride, rebellion, passion
raise no head.

Give me to know that heaven is all joy,
the end of believing, fasting, praying,
mourning, humbling, watching,
fearing, repining;

And lead me to it soon.[2]

Glorious God,

It is the flame of my life to worship thee,
the crown and glory of my soul to adore thee,
heavenly pleasure to approach thee.

Give me power by thy Spirit to help me
worship now,
that I may forget the world,
be brought into fullness of life,
be refreshed, comforted, blessed.

Give me knowledge of thy goodness
that I might not be over-awed by thy greatness;

Give me Jesus, Son of Man, Son of God,
that I might not be terrified,
but be drawn near with filial love,
with holy boldness;

He is my Mediator, Brother, Interpreter,
Branch, Daysman, Lamb;
him I glorify,
in him I am set on high.

Crowns to give I have none,

2. Bennett, *Valley of Vision*, 370–71.

> but what thou hast given I return,
> content to feel that everything is mine
> when it is thine,
> and the more fully mine when I have yielded it
> to thee.
>
> Let me live wholly to my Saviour,
> free from distractions,
> from carking care,
> from hindrances to the pursuit
> of the narrow way.
>
> I am pardoned through the blood of Jesus
> —give me a new sense of it,
> continue to pardon me by it,
> may I come every day to the fountain,
> and every day be washed anew,
> that I may worship thee always
> in spirit and truth.[3]

These prayers paint vivid imagery of how heavenly worship was anticipated by the Puritans of the eighteenth century. The Puritan perspective weighs heavily on *forgetting the world*, perhaps one of the valuable considerations when imagining heavenly worship. The tenor of these prayers is invaluable to church leaders who plan worship. The question arises as to how we use earthly creativity to capture these images. How can we as musicians and liturgists capture these images of heaven for the worshippers that come into our churches?

Apostles' Creed

Similarly, the Apostles' Creed from the fourth century, which so succinctly communicates the tenants of the Christian faith, climaxes with the ascension of Christ to heaven, where he sits on the right hand of the Father, and where we will enjoy *life everlasting*.

> I believe in God, the Father almighty,
> creator of heaven and earth.
>
> I believe in Jesus Christ, his only Son, our Lord,
> who was conceived by the Holy Spirit,

3. Ibid., 123.

born of the Virgin Mary,
suffered under Pontius Pilate,
was crucified, died, and was buried;
he descended to the dead.

On the third day he rose again;
he ascended into heaven,
he is seated at the right hand of the Father,
and he will come to judge the living and the dead.

I believe in the Holy Spirit,
the holy catholic Church,
the communion of saints,
the forgiveness of sins,
the resurrection of the body,
and the life everlasting.

Amen.

Here, the longstanding *Symbol of the Apostles* emphasizes the eternal aspect of hope in Christian living: living in heaven with God the Father and his Son Jesus Christ.

Westminster Confession of Faith

We will quickly see in chapter 21 of the Westminster Confession of Faith that thoughtful guidance regarding worship as offered by our forefathers of faith is regulated in the elements of worship that focus on God's vast domain.

Chapter XXI of Religious Worship and the Sabbath-Day

The light of nature showeth that there is a God, who hath lordship and sovereignty over all; is good, and doeth good unto all; and is therefore to be feared, loved, praised, called upon, trusted in, and served with all the hearth, and with all the soul, and with all the might. But the acceptable way of worshipping the true God is instituted by himself, and so limited by his own revealed will, that he may not be worshipped according to the imaginations and devices of men, or the suggestions of Satan, under any visible representation or any other way not prescribed in the holy Scripture.

1. Religious worship is to be given to God, the Father, Son, and Holy Ghost; and to him alone: not to angels, saints, or any other creature: and since the Fall, not without a Mediator; nor in the mediation of any other but of Christ alone.

2. Prayer with thanksgiving, being one special part of religious worship, is by God required of all men; and that it may be accepted, it is to be made in the name of the Son, by the help of his Holy Spirit, according to his will, with understanding, reverence, humility, fervency, faith, love, and perseverance; and, if vocal, in a known tongue.

3. Prayer is to be made for things lawful, and for all sorts of men living, or that shall live hereafter; but not for the dead, nor for those of whom it may be known that they have sinned the sin unto death.

4. The reading of the Scriptures with godly fear; the sound preaching, and conscionable hearing of the Word, in obedience unto God with understanding, faith, and reverence; singing of psalms with grace in the heart; as, also, the due administration and worthy receiving of the sacraments instituted by Christ; are all parts of the ordinary religious worship of God: besides religious oaths, and vows, solemn fastings, and thanksgivings upon special occasion; which are, in their several times and seasons, to be used in an holy and religious manner.

5. Neither prayer, nor any other part of religious worship, is now, under the gospel, either tied unto, or made more acceptable to, any place in which it is performed, or towards which it is directed: but God is to be worshipped everywhere in spirit and in truth; as in private families daily, and in secret each one by himself, so more solemnly in the public assemblies, which are not carelessly or willfully to be neglected or forsaken, when God, by his Word or providence, calleth thereunto.

6. As it is of the law of nature, that, in general, a due proportion of time be set apart for the worship of God; so, in his Word, by a positive, moral, and perpetual commandment, binding all men in all ages, he hath particularly appointed one day in seven for a Sabbath, to be kept holy unto him: which, from the beginning of the world to the resurrection of Christ, was the last day of the week; and, from the resurrection of Christ, was changed into the first day of the week, which in Scripture is called the Lord's Day, and is to be continued to the end of the world as the Christian Sabbath.

7. This Sabbath is to be kept holy unto the Lord when men, after a due preparing of their hearts, and ordering of their common affairs beforehand, do not only observe an holy rest all the day from their own works, words, and thoughts about their worldly employments and recreations; but also are taken up the whole time in the public and private exercises of his worship, and in the duties of necessity and mercy.[4]

The only instruction offered explicitly from the confession on music is to sing psalms. While this book is not a defense of exclusively utilizing psalmody, the Puritans were certainly known for their devotion to the psalms and many denominations throughout the world still adhere to exclusive singing of psalms in worship. However, for the rest of us in the evangelical church, this should serve as a reminder from, not only the Westminster Confession, but from Scripture itself, of the necessity to sing psalms, hymns, and spiritual songs.

The implicit language from the Confession shows us the devotion and awe that was a part of corporate worship. Without an exhaustive understanding of what music and worship were like in seventeenth-century England, it may be easy to assume that issues of worship we face today were of no concern at this time in history. While the issues may be different, some are similar. This was a time when music was developing rapidly. The development of polyphony (harmony) in church had been a new and unsettling issue for some. The use of instruments was still a question being debated. Amidst these musical issues in the church, it was a time of great forethought, creativity, and progression for music and theology, alike. What is clear from the Confession is the commitment to biblical truth, reverence, and awe.

John Calvin on Singing

John T. Dyke wrote an excellent analysis of John Calvin's outlook on singing. Calvin interprets Scripture's teachings on singing as warrant for our real vocal song, not just "singing in the heart." Calvin says, "We ought also to sing from the heart, that there may not be merely an external sound with the mouth. At the same time, we must not understand it as though he would have every one sing inwardly to himself, but he would have both

---

4. Westminster Confession of Faith, chapter 8.

conjoined, provided the heart goes before the tongue."[5] Calvin gives several reasons to sing, rather than merely speak, God's praises. But first, note that Calvin clarifies what is *not* a reason to sing:

> We sing in order to give him thanks—and not in order to produce a solemn ceremony as a meritorious work that we do for God. Those who take this approach are reverting to a sort of Jewishism, as if they wanted to mingle the law and the gospel, and thus bury our Lord Jesus Christ.[6]

Above all, Calvin insists on singing God's praises for two complimentary reasons: gratitude to the Savior and obligation to the Lord. First,

> He singles out the divine mercy and truth as the subject of his praise, for while the power and greatness of God are equally worthy of commendation, nothing has a more sensible influence in stimulating us to thanksgiving than his free mercy; and in communicating to us of his goodness he opens our mouth to sing his praises.[7]

And also,

> It is indeed the duty of all men to sing praise to God, for there is no person who is not bound to it by the strongest obligations; but more lofty praises ought to proceed from those on whom more valuable gifts have been bestowed. Now, since God has laid open the fountain of all blessings in Christ, and has displayed all spiritual riches, we need not wonder if he demand that we offer to him an unwonted and excellent sacrifice of praise.[8]

Beyond this, Calvin gives many other motivations for singing, such as in response to the consolation of God's sovereignty: "His divine power ought justly to strike terror into the wicked, so it is described as full of the sweetest consolation to us, which ought to inspire us with joy, and incite us to celebrate it with songs of praise and thanksgivings." We should sing for God's faithful promises: "When, therefore, the Prophets bade the Church to sing to God and to give thanks, they thus confirmed the promises made to them . . . therefore they could boldly join in a song of thanks to God, as though they were already enjoying full redemption; for the Lord will perfect what he begins." More pragmatically, singing is for mutual edification:

5. Dyck, "Calvin and Worship," 33–34.
6. Calvin, Commentary, Col 3:16; 2 Sam 6:1–7.
7. Ibid.
8. Ibid., Ps 138:2; Isa 42:10.

"Here we see the true use of hymns: we are to encourage one another to celebrate and magnify the name of God in our hymns (Eph. 5:19–20)." So great a priority was this for Calvin that of all the complaints he had with the church of Geneva when he arrived, he drew up four points of reform in the *Articles* of 1537, and one of them was,

> Further, it is a thing very expedient for the edification of the Church, to sing some psalms in the form of public devotions by which one may pray to God, or to sing his praise so that the hearts of all be roused and incited to make life prayers and render like praises and thanks to God with one accord.[9]

In addition, singing in worship is a more concentrated form of expression, and can therefore be an aid to worship:

> And surely, if the singing be tempered to that gravity which is fitting in the sight of God and the angels, it both lends dignity and grace to sacred actions and has the greatest value in kindling our hearts to a true zeal and eagerness to pray.[10]

Calvin calls on believers to follow the example of the early church and to avoid the distorted practice of the Roman Catholic Church:

> There are the psalms which we desire to be sung in the Church, as we have it exemplified in the ancient Church and in the evidence of Paul himself, who says it is good to sing in the congregation with mouth and heart . . . Moreover it will be thus appreciated of what benefit and consolation the pope and those that belong to him have deprived the Church.[11]

Another interesting motivation presented in the form of an argument for the singing of God's praises has its genesis in the fact that we are created the image of God.

> Moreover, since the glory of God ought, in a measure, to shine in the several parts of our bodies, it is especially fitting that the tongue has been assigned and destined for this task, both through singing and through speaking. For it was peculiarly created to tell and proclaim the praise of God.[12]

9. Ibid., Isa 5:12, 3.9.3.

10. Ibid.

11. Ibid. Ps 22:13; Zech 2:10; Serm. 2 Sam 6:1–7; Calvin, *Articles Concerning the Organization*, 3.20.32.

12. Calvin, *Institutes*, 3.20.31; Dyck, "Calvin and Worship," 33–34.

In other words, singing the praises of God is part of man's task in carrying out the moral perfection involved in the *imago Dei*.

John Calvin and the Regulative Principle

B. B. Warfield referred to John Calvin as "pre-eminently the theologian of the Holy Spirit."[13] This is because of Calvin's emphasis on the work of the Spirit as foundational to saving faith in believers. As a corollary to that statement we might also refer to Calvin as the "Theologian of Worship," even though he did not write very much specifically about worship. He understood that faith in Christ began with a change of heart, which necessarily led to worship and devotion.[14]

Calvin believed very strongly that it is not enough to acknowledge that God exists and to perform ceremonies for him. But very early in the *Institutes of the Christian Religion*, Calvin says:

> Moreover, although our mind cannot apprehend God without rendering some honor to him, it will not suffice simply to hold that there is one whom all ought to honor and adore, unless we are also persuaded that he is the fountain of every good, and that we must seek nothing elsewhere than in him."[15]Piety is essential to worship and he goes on to define it: "I call 'piety' that reverence joined with love of God which the knowledge of his benefits induces. For until men recognize that they owe everything to God, that they are nourished by his fatherly care, that he is the Author of their every good, that they should seek nothing beyond him— they will never yield him willing service. Nay, unless they establish their complete happiness in him, they will never give themselves truly and sincerely to him.[16]

The theological lessons and foundations from the early Reformers here are clear in their zeal and expectation for the standards of worship. By paralleling the sentiments expressed from these great men of faith and applying them to the practice of church music, we gain clear direction for the attitude, tenor, and high expectation of how music should be directed toward God. Nowhere do we find in these documents or writings how music

13. Warfield, *Calvin as a Theologian*, 23.

14. Dyck, "Calvin and Worship," 36.

15. Calvin, *Institutes*, 1:2:1.

16. Dyck, "Calvin and Worship," 33–40.

or any worship component is to be aimed at earthly expectations or for the benefit of the worshippers.

As we move forward to the twentieth and twenty-first centuries in the next chapter, we will see where our attitudes regarding church music shift—not only in style—but in intent, understanding, and practice of music in worship. The shift moves from an angle of clear intent for whom our worship music is created to a quasi-dual function of aiming toward heaven and earth simultaneously.

Summary of Church Music in the Last 2,000 Years

In their book, *Perimeters of Light,* Ed Stetzer and Elmer Towns summarize some of the monumental moments in the history of church music. The premise of their brief timeline is to point out the ongoing struggle over issues on matters of music and church.

> 200s: Instrumental music was almost universally shunned because of its association with debauchery and immorality. Lyre playing, for example, was associated with prostitution.

> 300s: Ambrose of Milan (339–397), an influential bishop often called the father of hymnody in the Western church, was the first to introduce community hymn-singing in the church. These hymns were composed in metrical stanzas, quite unlike biblical poetry. They did not rhyme but they were sometimes sung while marching. Many of these hymns took songs written by heretics, using the same meter but rewriting the words.

> 500s: Congregations often sang psalms in a way that "everyone responds." This probably involved the traditional Jewish practice of cantor and congregation singing alternate verses.

> 600s: The monasteries, referencing "Seven times a day I praise you" (Ps 119:164), developed a seven-times-daily order of prayer. The services varied in content, but included a certain amount of singing, mainly by a solo singer, with the congregation repeating a refrain at intervals. The services were linked together by their common basis in the biblical psalms in such a way that the whole cycle of 150 psalms was sung every week.

> 800s: Almost all singing was done in chant, based on scales that used only the white keys on today's piano. The monastery was the

setting above all others where Christian music was sustained and developed through the Dark Ages.

900s: Music began to be widely notated for the first time, enabling choirs to sing from music. Thus new types of music could be created which would have been quite out of the reach of traditions where music was passed on by ear.

1100s: The perfection of new forms of Latin verse using rhyme and accent led to new mystical meditations on the joys of heaven, the vanity of life, and the suffering of Christ.

1200s: Starting in France, musicians began to discover the idea of harmony. The startling effect of the choir suddenly changing from the lone and sinuous melody of the chant to two-, three-, or even four-part music did not please everyone. One critic commented how harmony sullied worship by introducing "lewdness" into church.

1300s: Worship in the great Gothic-era cathedrals and abbeys used choirs of paid professionals, "a church within a church," sealed off by screens from the greater building. Ordinary people generally had no place in the spiritual life of these great buildings, except perhaps in the giving of their finances.

1400s: Music became increasingly complex (Gothic sounds for Gothic buildings), prompting criticisms that only the choir was allowed to sing. As reformer John Wycliffe had complained, "No one can hear the words, and all the others are dumb and watch them like fools."

1500s: The new prayerbook, pushed by King Henry VIII of England decreed that all services would be in English, with only one syllable to each note.

1500s: Martin Luther set about reforming public worship by freeing the mass from what he believed to be rigid forms. One way he did this was by putting stress on congregational singing. He used hymns and music already familiar to the majority of people in Germany.

1600s: The organ played an important part in Lutheranism, Anglicanism, and Roman Catholicism, while in the Reformed churches there was much opposition to it. Initially the organ was not used to accompany congregational singing, but had its own voice. As a result, the organist would often play a verse on the congregation's behalf.

1700s: Isaac Watts gave a great boost to the controversial idea of a congregation singing "man-made" hymns, which he created by freely paraphrasing Scripture. Charles Wesley paraphrased the Prayer Book, and versified Christian doctrine and experience. Wesley's songs were said to have had at least a great as influence as his sermons.

1800s: William Booth, founder of The Salvation Army, used rousing melodies with a martial flavor to set the tone for his Army.

1900s: When radio was in its infancy, a handful of Christian pioneers such as Donald Grey Barnhouse and Charles E. Fuller began featuring gospel music and evangelistic teaching over the airwaves. Many Christians initially showed skepticism.

1970s: Larry Norman sang, "I want the people to know, That He saved my soul, But I still like to listen to the radio . . . They say that rock and roll is wrong . . . I know what's right, I know what's wrong and I don't confuse it: Why should the devil have all the good music . . . "Cause Jesus is the Rock and He rolled my blues away." He founded what became known as Contemporary Christian Music . . . and it is still controversial today.[17]

So, what have we learned through all of this? What are the musical implications for the modern church musician in a time with all of this knowledge and available material? Perhaps it is time to look at music in the church from a different perspective. The development of music, commercialization, information dispersal, and marketing have certainly shaped worship in the past thousand years. With the change of music also has come change in the ways the church operates: the social structure, the government, the methodology in which we worship, evangelize, and minister. These have developed to create what in America has become the epitome of how the world, and especially Christians, view the church. We have modeled ministry after corporations, social organizations, and governmental hierarchy. The result has put the American church in a place of uncertainty and unrest.

Let us think about how we can move forward with a *heavenly* look, while looking back at what we have learned. This approach is, perhaps, looking backwards to get to our roots, in order to gain heavenly (future) perspective. Of course, as the old saying *don't throw the baby out with the bath water* reminds us, we have much to gain from 2,000 years of practices in the development of Christ's church.

17. Stetzer and Towns, *Perimeters of Light*, 112.

CHAPTER 4

Present Church Worship

Our God, our help in ages past,
Our hope for years to come,
Our shelter from the stormy blast,
And our eternal home.

Under the shadow of Thy throne
Thy saints have dwelt secure;
Sufficient is Thine arm alone,
And our defense is sure.

Before the hills in order stood,
Or earth received her frame,
From everlasting Thou art God,
To endless years the same.

A thousand ages in Thy sight
Are like an evening gone;
Short as the watch that ends the night
Before the rising sun.

Time, like an ever rolling stream,
Bears all its sons away;
They fly, forgotten, as a dream
Dies at the opening day.

—ISAAC WATTS

To LOOK AT THE corporate worship practices of the past century in the United States, we must consider the variety of worship experiences that have been a part of the fabric of churches. Unlike any other era, continent, or within a given religion, we have seen more diversity among church music than ever. The development of communication, recorded music, and an industry centered on music have contributed to these influences in the church.

In 1964, British church musician and author Erik Routley wrote: "In church music there has been no age so full of surprises, and so full of creative promise, as our own. I should stand by this hazardous judgment in the face of any defender of the sixteenth century."[1] He goes on to say, "church music is receiving more serious attention from musicians of proved excellence than it has since the time of Palestrina (court musician for the Pope in the sixteenth century)."[2] He goes on to speak of the excellent ways these *serious contemporary* church musicians such as Benjamin Britten and Eric Thiman are contributing. These are fine composers of whom most people within the American evangelical church have never heard. The creative promise was coming from church musicians who were a product of the previous generation and were considered to be the pinnacle of their era. The continued development of church music is ever-changing and we are to carry on the narrative as passed down from our previous generations. The opportunities are vast, choices are many, and issues of concern are broad.

Lifted Up With the Ascended Christ: Holy Communion on Earth

At once I was in the Spirit, and behold, a throne stood in heaven, with one seated on the throne.

—REVELATION 4:2

Before looking at the aspects of music in our worship on earth, we need to look at the role of communion (the Lord's Supper, Holy Eucharist) in instituting heaven on earth for Christ's followers. With the renewed emphasis on communion within our evangelical churches, it is important to

---

1. Routley, *Twentieth Century Church Music*, 7.
2. Ibid., 8.

look at the present through means in which we are being transformed in our Christian lives.

Heavenly worship occurs during the celebration of the ancient liturgy as the people of God, lifted up to heaven with the ascended Christ, partake of communion. The Holy Eucharist unites heaven and earth by elevating the church into an experience of worship with the people of God, past and present, around the throne of God, and in the presence of God. Heavenly worship recognizes that the line between the physical reality of earth and the spiritual reality of heaven will become blurred as we enter the presence of the Lamb of God, slain yet standing, on the altar of God.

The worship that we experience on earth should be an experience of the worship that is presently occurring in heaven. Not only should heavenly worship be our experience, but our models of worship should reflect those elements of worship used in heaven. Biblical instruction direct the people of God to worship following the model and practices of heaven. Earthly worship is to mirror heavenly worship in "spirit and in truth."[3]

> In order that pious souls may duly apprehend Christ in the supper, they may be raised up to heaven . . . and for the same reason it was established of old that before the consecration the people should be told in a loud voice to lift up their hearts.[4]

And, we can look to Orthodox and Catholic congregations to see their deep understanding on communing not only with one another on earth, but with all the company of heaven.

> We knew not whether we were in heaven or on earth. Worship, for the Orthodox Church, is nothing less than "heaven on earth." The Holy Liturgy is something that embraces two worlds at once, for both in heaven and on earth the liturgy is one and the same—one altar, one sacrifice, one presence. In every place of worship, however humble its outward appearance, as the faithful gather to perform the Eucharist, they are taken up into the "heavenly places"; in every place of worship when the holy sacrifice is offered, not merely the local congregation is present, but the church universal—the saints, the angels . . . and Christ himself.[5]

---

3. Exod 24:9–11; Isa 6:1–5; Ezek 1:4–28; Dan 7:9–14; Heb 12:22–24; Rev 4:1—5:14.

4. Calvin, *Institutes*, 4.17.36.

5. Ware, "The Earthly Heaven," 12.

As evangelical Protestants, and especially among our Reformed communities, we have experienced a renewal of the role of the communion feast as a force drawing us into the heavenly community of worship. As this understanding grows, and as many churches move from low-church orders of worship (or liturgies) to high-church liturgies that draw the believers into the dialogue between God and his people, I pray that we will also rethink our attitudes of how our music can align and enhance our earthly expressions of worship. The parallel between the Holy Eucharist and the praises and prayers offered through worship music can ascend our spirits to that of our ascended Lord.

Corporate and Individual Experience

Worship is shaped by society and culture based on common experience. It should therefore be shaped by the highest standards within that culture. Our global society is becoming more connected and therefore has many options for determining means of communicating the elements and language of worship. As a result, our common experience is expanding beyond our local communities. Our experience is both corporate and individual. For Presbyterians and many other evangelical churches, our experience as a faith is rooted in historical theology, which holds firm and maintains its relevance in our churches to this day. Our experience has been one that has held high regard for worship and the approach to God. Presbyterianism in particular has enjoyed an age of rich hymnody and strong congregational singing because of the emphasis on text and melody. It is important to understand what the church can do corporately, rather than individually—the transformation power of corporate worship that we cannot experience on our own. John Piper challenges us in the importance of what we do corporately on Sundays:

> Nothing makes God more supreme and more central than when a
> people are utterly persuaded that nothing—not money or prestige
> or leisure or family or job or health or sports or toys or friends—
> is going to bring satisfaction to their aching hearts besides God.
> This conviction breeds a people who passionately long for God on
> Sunday morning. They are not confused about why they are here.
> They do not see songs and prayers and sermons as mere traditions

or mere duties. They see them as means of getting to God or God getting to them for more of His fullness.[6]

The church certainly must consider matters of music and worship in the corporate aspect—the importance of how worship communicates to all races, generations, and backgrounds. Rather than looking to our cultural or generational patterns, perhaps we should model worship to better equip us for what we will experience together with all the hosts of saints and angels, corporately, in heaven. There is no doubt that corporate worship should be *a grand practice for heaven.*

The Individual Christian Journey

Worship is first and foremost for His benefit, not ours, though it is marvelous to discover that in giving Him pleasure, we ourselves enter into what can become our richest and most wholesome experience in life.

—LAMAR BOSCHMAN[7]

Each individual's story is different as to how believers experience the love of God and the pace of that unique journey. In most cases, the journey begins with an intense hunger for every drop of teaching and lessons in Christian living possible. As we continue to grow in faith, we experience the benefit of having real life experiences, and fortunately, a new method in dealing with the basic struggles of life. Likewise, a new Christian may yearn for a basic approach to worship that instantly helps one feel in the presence of God. They want worship to feel comfortable to them—familiar. However, we have seen that as the journey of the Christian life changes, so does the expectation of what we desire as an individual to offer God. Therefore, it is no doubt that what a new Christian may experience in corporate worship would be very different from that of one who has followed Christ for many years.

So how does the church meet the needs of all worshippers, new and old alike? How do we adequately plan words and music to express the sentiment of a seasoned believer at the same time as one who joined the faith last week? Historically, this has been simple: immersion into a culture. Just as linguists would say the best way to learn a new language is to be immersed

6. Piper, *Brothers*, 239.

7. Boschman, *A Heart For Worship*, 58.

into the constant use of that language, the same applies to growing in an intimate relationship and understanding of God. The more one experiences the blessings of God in life, the more the corporate worship of experienced Christians makes sense. To simplify the corporate worship of Christians for the sake of the new or immature Christian is a disservice to the church and it promotes among all a lower expectation for Christian growth. Christian living thrives on curiosity, personal application, and striving for deeper knowledge of God's truth—all this we gain by being challenged in corporate worship.

The Corporate Christian Journey

C. S. Lewis aptly said, "we only learn to behave ourselves in the presence of God."[8] Worship is transformational, not experiential. Current worship trends are usually based on an experience, rather than a transforming act of learning, or practicing, to be in the presence of God. The more the church strives to bring relevance to the culture by stripping away vocabulary, verbal and musical, the more we lower the bar for the expectation of Christian growth. The corporate church worship service should not be afraid to maintain an intellectual approach to faith. Regardless of one's intellectual ability, a faith in God must be centered around the Bible. This requires an ability to study and interpret Scripture. Whether we interpret the Scripture ourselves or lean on the work of theologians, scholars, or pastors, we require some level of intellectual activity to process the teaching of Scripture and its application to life. Calvin speaks to the value of the intellect in the aim of singing with understanding.

> . . . the spiritual songs cannot be well sung save from the heart. But the heart requires the intelligence. And in that (says St. Augustine) lies the difference between the singing of men and that of the birds. For a linnet, a nightingale, a parrot may sing well; but it will be without understanding. But the unique gift of man is to sing knowing that which he sings. After the intelligence must follow the heart and the affection, a thing which is unable to be except if we have the hymn imprinted on our memory, in order never to cease from singing . . . But that the world may be so well advised, that in place of songs in part vain and frivolous, in part stupid and dull, in part foul and vile, and in consequence evil and harmful

8. Lewis, *Mere Christianity*, 58.

which it has used up to now, it may accustom itself hereafter to the
singing of these divine and celestial hymns with the good king David. Touching the melody, it has seemed best that it be moderated
in the manner we have adopted to carry the weight and majesty
appropriate to the subject, and even to be proper for singing in the
Church, according to that which has been said.[9]

So, for one to categorize corporate worship as overly intellectual or
too complicated is in direct contradiction of the basic premise that the
Christian faith is one of continual growth and an aspiration of deeper
understanding of Scripture. The worship service should not only be the
pinnacle of our worship, but also be the highest challenge for deeper spiritual knowledge. To separate growing in truth from that of worship presents
major questions. If we seek to glorify God to the best of our ability, should
this not include the language we use to give adoration to God? Whereas we
may feel that our language in worship does not matter, God may see that
the intellect we gain on our journey has helped us better express ourselves
to him in worship and prayer.

Thus, the challenge is coordinating a corporate worship service in a
time and place where many socioeconomic, racial, cultural, and education-
al backgrounds worship together as a family. This is certainly a beautiful
picture of heaven, isn't it? However, it presents a huge challenge for those
who plan a time of worship. Even as Christianity spreads throughout the
world, we see these questions being asked.

> The gospel transforms personal and corporate lives, and worship
> is the proper response to God's grace. Whatever the immense
> cultural and social diversity found within worldwide Christianity,
> one thing holds true: Christians worship.[10]

Farhadian continues to introduce the growing numbers of Christians
in the southern hemisphere and how the Christian faith is becoming increasingly "non-Western." In an attempt to answer the question "How do
Christians worship worldwide 'in the meantime,' in mystery and anticipation," he says

> Christian worship is always partly open to surprises; it is never
> complete. In worship, Christians take baby steps toward some-
> thing eternal, full of substance and permanency. Perhaps this is

9. Calvin, *Geneva Psalter*, preface.

10. Farhadian, *Christian Worship Worldwide*, 2.

what Michael Polanyi means when he writes that Christian worship "sustains, as it were, an eternal. Never to be a consummated hunch: a heuristic vision which is accepted for the sake of its unresolvable tension."[11]

Worship necessarily entails qualities of mystery and knowledge. The sacraments serve, in St. Augustine's apt phrase, as an "outward and visible sign of an inward and spiritual grace." Failure to recognize this element of mystery can easily lull the assembly into self-worship, where a community's own culture and lifeways become the focus and end of worship. On the other hand, worship must be meaningful to worshippers, or it inevitably becomes directed toward something other than its intended focus—God.

> ... as such, Christian worship is inherently political, since it entails people giving glory to God and not earthly powers. Many of the earliest Christians were tortured, harassed, and put to death because of their insistence that the living God was to be worshipped above Caesar. The same is true today in many non-Western regions. Being witnesses continues to be a central theme in the worldwide Christian movement. Christian worship invigorates life "in the meantime," as glimpses of redemption and reconciliation of all creation inspire reconciliation with God and other human communities.[12] Christian worship is inseparable from its wider social impact.[13]

The realities mentioned here are real life issues that we must consider when sitting comfortably in our cozy American or other civilized society churches. The worship communicates to the social culture, but needs not to conform to it. This is widely recognizable in places where Christianity is forbidden among the culture. The churches continue to worship boldly, sometimes against the laws of the governing powers. This is certainly a countercultural approach to worship, and in that sense, is counter-earthly. Could this be deduced as heavenward focused worship because it is functioning against the ways of the world. I would say yes.

We could go on to say that the corporate worship of God's people is transformational even, when being carried out amid tension or persecution from the world. This could be presumed with an analysis of most biblical, historical, and global instances where worship of God carried on, even

11. Polanyi, *Personal Knowledge*, 199.

12. See Rom 8:18–25.

13. Farhadian, *Christian Worship Worldwide*, 4.

against the earthly rule or powers that existed. Again, this is difficult to understand in our American church society. So, what does this have to do with music, worship, or the corporate body gathered for Sunday worship? Perhaps the answer is found in Scripture, from the Apostle Paul:

> I appeal to you therefore, brothers, by the mercies of God, to present your bodies as a living sacrifice, holy and acceptable to God, which is your spiritual worship. Do not be conformed to this world, but be transformed by the renewal of your mind, that by testing you may discern what is the will of God, what is good and acceptable and perfect.[14]

This is quite a challenge for the church today. Paul certainly understood persecution and carried out his ministry under dire opposition from the world. We could simply apply our heavenly model or vision as an alternative to any cultural or stylistic preference our modern churches attach themselves. The opportunity for corporate worship to be associated with heaven, rather than any earthly produced models, could perhaps void the issues of style, choices of music, cultural barriers, use of language, or lack of depth, and the like. Even as our cultural differences give identity to our various churches, they should be secondary, and our primary identity should be as a church that is committed to the types of biblical and historical transformation we have seen up to this point.

Style and Personal Preference

Many of the current issues regarding worship and church music are derived from themes associated with the information age and the individual and narcissistic lifestyles that are commonplace in most developed countries. The current issues seem to revolve more around the individual rather then the church as a whole, or even the church universal. Drastic pressure on churches to "change with the times," has given birth to a plethora of ideas of how worship should be done. The "style" of worship has been the determining factor for many when "church shopping" in the twenty-first century. The "personal preference" of music, preacher, or space to worship has become the intrigue of church leaders around the world. Many studies and much research is done each year to determine "what the next generation" wants in worship.

14. Rom 12:1–12.

While many church leaders clamor to find new ways to keep people in their congregations engaged and thinking about religion, many others "carry on" about traditions and methods that have been a part of church life for hundreds of years. While we can look at trends, study data, and develop more research, perhaps going back to the basics of Christianity is in order. Perhaps a realignment of thought on to whom worship is directed could transform our leadership and personal worship in the modern church.

> In a day when many Christians operate as spiritual entrepreneurs, it is important to remember that we do not decide how to come to God (or "connect," "experience," "encounter" or whichever word is popular). [The] goal of authentic worship is the glory of God rather than the pleasure of human beings, which means that forms of worship should conform to the will of God rather than to the whims of fallen humanity.[15]

While music is highly subjective, a good start at evaluating how to look towards heavenly worship could be as simple as working from within our own context to discover how we can plan our worship on a "heavenly" scale.

The Ceremony of Corporate Worship

One way I have personally seen how people think about church music and worship is when it comes to planning a wedding. I have met with many families in planning weddings where a desire for the very best and most highly cultured music is desired. Our church has several church plants that meet in buildings other than a traditional church building. We allow many of these church partners to use our sanctuary for their weddings. The first observation is their desire for an architectural aesthetic that their church may not offer. They want their special day to be in an opulent setting. In many cases, the parallel of worshipping in such a space is against their instincts, and thus they want to be in a church that is closely similar to their world, or culture, rather than different from it. Similarly, during the process of planning music with the bride, they most often request music that is very stately and grand, classical and high—very different from the worship services they normally attend.

---

15. Pruitt, "Is Your Worship Christian or Pagan?" para 3; Block, *For the Glory of God*, 6.

Likewise, we see grand pageantry in many of our American cultural and social institutions. The elaborate expense and display in school functions, such as graduations and proms, corporate parties, and anniversary parties, where we are expected to dress up and put on our best, is not foreign to our American culture. It has, however, slipped away from our associations with church worship.

So, why then would we use music in a worship service with different expectations than those of our own earthly wedding celebrations, graduations and other ceremonies and celebrations? Each time we worship our God it should be a feast as grand as any earthly or heavenly wedding or feast. The expectation of standards while on earth has been driving much of the church's discontent over music. And, again, the issue of narcissism, and lack of deep understanding about worship create these types of misalignments and contradictions within our Christian culture of America, usually unknowingly. We all have preferences that become accentuated the more we cater to personal desire. The case of music style in the church can be easily remedied if we develop a philosophy founded in creating music that is for God's glory and is modeled toward a heavenly expectation.

CHAPTER 5

Future Worship: Heaven

*After this I heard what seemed to be the loud voice of a great
multitude in heaven crying out. Hallelujah!*

—REVELATION 19:1

THE IMAGERY FOUND WITHIN the book of Revelation paints a glorious
picture of corporate worship. It can serve as a model and as inspiration
for our own corporate worship music. Though there are many wonderful
intimate and tender moments of private worship displayed throughout the
Bible, the depictions of heavenly worship are breathtaking. Let's look at a
few examples:

> He came and took the scroll from the right hand of him who sat
> on the throne. And when he had taken it, the four living creatures
> and the twenty-four elders fell down before the Lamb. Each one
> had a harp and they were holding golden bowls full of incense,
> which are the prayers of the saints. And they sang a new song:
> "You are worthy to take the scroll and to open its seals, because
> you were slain, and with your blood you purchased men for God
> from every tribe and language and people and nation. You have
> made them to be a kingdom and priests to serve our God, and
> they will reign on the earth." Then I looked and heard the voice
> of many angels, numbering thousands upon thousands, and ten
> thousand times ten thousand. They encircled the throne and the
> living creatures and the elders. In a loud voice they sang: "Worthy
> is the Lamb, who was slain, to receive power and wealth and wis-
> dom and strength and honor and glory and praise!" Then I heard

every creature in heaven and on earth and under the earth and on the sea, and all that is in them, singing: "To him who sits on the throne and to the Lamb be praise and honor and glory and power, for ever and ever!" The four living creatures said, "Amen," and the elders fell down and worshiped.[1]

Then I looked, and there before me was the Lamb, standing on Mount Zion, and with him 144,000 who had his name and his Father's name written on their foreheads. And I heard a sound from heaven like the roar of rushing waters and like a loud peal of thunder. The sound I heard was like that of harpists playing their harps. And they sang a new song before the throne and before the four living creatures and the elders. No one could learn the song except the 144,000 who had been redeemed from the earth. These are those who did not defile themselves with women, for they kept themselves pure. They follow the Lamb wherever he goes. They were purchased from among men and offered as firstfruits to God and the Lamb.[2]

I saw in heaven another great and marvelous sign: seven angels with the seven last plagues—last, because with them God's wrath is completed. And I saw what looked like a sea of glass mixed with fire and, standing beside the sea, those who had been victorious over the beast and his image and over the number of his name. They held harps given them by God and sang the song of Moses the servant of God and the song of the Lamb: "Great and marvelous are your deeds, Lord God Almighty. Just and true are your ways, King of the ages. Who will not fear you, O Lord, and bring glory to your name? For you alone are holy. All nations will come and worship before you, for your righteous acts have been revealed."[3]

Then a mighty angel picked up a boulder the size of a large millstone and threw it into the sea, and said: "With such violence the great city of Babylon will be thrown down, never to be found again. The music of harpists and musicians, flute players and trumpeters, will never be heard in you again. No workman of any trade will ever be found in you again. The sound of a millstone will never be heard in you again. The light of a lamp will never shine in you again. The voice of bridegroom and bride will never be heard in

1. Rev 5:7, NIV.

2. Rev 14:1.

3. Rev 15:1.

you again. Your merchants were the world's great men. By your magic spell all the nations were led astray.[4]

Every Creature in Heaven
and Earth is Worshipping Now

And every creature which is in the heaven and upon the earth and under the earth, and those that are upon the sea, and all things in them, heard I saying, To him that sits upon the throne, and to the Lamb, blessing, and honor, and glory, and might, to the ages of *ages*.[5]

Often when we think of the book of Revelation, we think future: second coming, final judgment, and the new heavens and new earth. However, the events in the book of Revelation have happened, are happening, and will happen.[6] These unusual and spectacular events happened in the first century. Revelation speaks today to churches oppressed and persecuted by mighty governments who claim absolute, almost religious, authority over every citizen in their realm. The book of Revelation also contains insights into eternity that speak of Christ's visible return in glory and the experience of eternal life in God's presence.

Revelation chapters 4 and 5 reveal to us the great throne of God. The throne is a symbol of the sovereign majesty of the King. The world may be in turmoil, but God reigns: he is defeating his foes, expanding his kingdom, and overcoming Satan's wiles. Around the throne, all manner of heavenly creatures, elders, angels, and humans worship and declare their praises of the Holy One and the Lamb.

The door to heavenly worship[7] is open as we "join our voices with angels and archangels and with all the company of heaven"[8] to praise and worship the Holy One and the Lamb for their holiness,[9] for creation,[10] for New

4. Rev 18:21.

5. Rev 5:13.

6. Rev 5:16.

7. Rev 4:1.

8. Book of Common Prayer (1972), 362.

9. Rev 5:8.

10. Rev 4:11.

Covenant blessing,[11] for Calvary's victory,[12] and for their unity.[13] Around the table of the Lord, the church is given a grand invitation to be lifted up into the heavenly places[14] and to experience now the joy of eternal worship.

> In the earthly liturgy we take part in a foretaste of that heavenly liturgy which is celebrated in the holy city of Jerusalem toward which we journey as pilgrims, where Christ is sitting at the right hand of God, a minister of the holies and of the true tabernacle; we sing a hymn to the Lord's glory with all the warriors of the heavenly army; venerating the memory of the saints, we hope for some part and fellowship with them; we eagerly await the Savior, Our Lord Jesus Christ, until He, our life, shall appear and we too will appear with Him in glory.[15]

Music in the Book of Revelation

Craig Koester in *The Distant Triumph Song: Music and the Book of Revelation* opens with a very secular viewpoint of what heaven will be like. Mark Twain considered scenes of the saints ceaselessly singing and playing their harps in heaven to be among the most ludicrous imaginings of the human mind. His reasoning was simple: such a heaven would contain nothing that human beings actually value. To be more specific,

> "Most men do not sing, most men cannot sing, most men will not stay where others are singing if it be continued more than two hours." Yet in heaven everyone is expected to sing all day every day without respite, and the music is invariably one of the same dozen or so hymns. Moreover, every one is supposed to play a harp, "whereas not more than twenty in the thousand of them could play an instrument in the earth, or ever wanted to." Multiply this by the millions and millions of voices in heaven and the prospect is a cacophony of gargantuan proportions.[16]

Twain's remarks are aimed in large part at the book of Revelation, which is the source for many of the popular images of heaven, from the

11. Rev 5:9–10.

12. Rev 5:12.

13. Rev 5:13.

14. Eph 1:3.

15. Constitution on the Sacred Liturgy 8, The Council of Vatican II.

16. Twain, *Letters from the Earth*, 321.

strains of angelic harp music to the splendor of the pearly gates. His satirical commentary aptly points out how readily Revelation's portrayal of the celestial chorus can be reduced to sentimentality, challenging us to rediscover the depth and power of this material. Music plays a larger role in the book of Revelation than in any other book of the New Testament, and few books in all of Scripture have spawned more hymns sung in Christian worship today. Attention to how the hymnic material in Revelation would have sounded to the Christians who first heard it, to the place of these hymns in Revelation as a whole, and to their relation to the rest of Scripture can help revitalize the singing of the hymns these passages have inspired.[17]

Songs of a Disputed Authority

The story begins on the island of Patmos in the Aegean Sea, where a visionary named John had been forcibly interned. The book of Revelation is a letter that he penned to seven churches on the mainland.[18] In the second and third chapters of the letter, John surveyed the conditions of these congregations, which were scattered throughout the Roman province of Asia, delineating the threats confronting each of them:

1. a seductive form of false teaching, which encouraged Christians to assimilate more fully into Roman society by eating meat sacrificed to idols, plagued congregations in the region's leading city, Ephesus; the provincial capital, Pergamum; and the important commercial center, Thyatira;

2. conflict with local synagogues and the specter of being denounced to the provincial authorities and suffering possible imprisonment or death loomed over Christians at Smyrna and Philadelphia;

3. complacency, born from the prosperity fostered by the Roman economic system, sapped the vitality from the faith of the Christians at Sardis and Laodicea.[19]

The sound of a trumpet-like voice in Revelation 4:1 heralded the beginning of a new scene that confronted Christians in all these situations with a vision of God on the throne. He was cloaked with a rainbow and a

---

17. Koester, "The Distant Triumph Song," 244.

18. Rev 1:4, 9–11.

19. Collins, *Crisis and Catharsis*, chs. 3–4.

sea of glass stretched before his feet. Four fantastic creatures, full of eyes in front and behind, and twenty-four elders dressed in white attended him. Lightning flashed, thunder roared, and from the mouths of the creatures burst forth—a song. And "day and night they never cease to sing, 'Holy, holy, holy, is the Lord God Almighty.'"[20] The twenty-four elders were caught up into the music and cast down their golden crowns before the throne. Bowing down, they joined in singing, "Worthy art thou, our Lord and God, to receive glory and honor and power."[21]

The chorus of praise was soon interrupted by the voice of an angel, calling for the One who is worthy to open the seals of the scroll held by the hand of God.[22] Moments later a Lamb appeared, "as though it had been slain." When the Lamb stepped forward, the thundering songs of praise began anew, as the creatures and the elders acclaimed him worthy to take the scroll and break its seals, because by his blood he had ransomed people from every tribe and tongue and people and nation.[23] The music swelled as myriads of angels joined in singing "Worthy is the Lamb who was slain, to receive power and wealth and wisdom and might and honor and glory and blessing."[24] Then music exploded into a cosmic chorus of praise, as every creature in heaven and on earth and every living thing under the earth and in the sea added their voices to the worship of God and the Lamb.[25]

These songs, which beckon readers to join in the chorus, are the songs of a disputed sovereignty.[26] The Lord God reigns, but not without opposition. The identity of the rival to the throne would have been all too clear to Christians in the Roman province of Asia. Caesar had his own throne and was attended by his own collection of dignitaries. Those who approached him were to bow in humble adoration, and delegations from the communities in his far-flung empire would offer him crowns of gold. Courtiers were notorious for keeping up a perpetual chorus of praise, lauding him day and night with appellations ordinarily reserved for deities. The current emperor, Domitian, exceeded the hubris of his predecessors by claiming for himself precisely the titles "Lord and God." Imperial propaganda and

20. Rev 4:8.

21. Rev 4:11.

22. Rev 5:1–2.

23. Rev 4:9.

24. Rev 5:12.

25. Rev 5:13.

26. Koester, "The Distant Triumph Song," 246.

popular oratory stressed the magnitude of the emperor's achievements and the acclaim awarded him by peoples everywhere.[27]

Christians who echoed the celestial refrains in their own earthly worship were confessing that sovereignty belonged to God and the Lamb, and not to any other aspirant to the throne. The implications for the seven churches in Asia were manifold:

1. the songs gave voice to a singular loyalty that countered tendencies to assimilate comfortably into the idolatry of the surrounding culture;

2. the songs announced that the creative and redeeming power of God and the Lamb would endure forever, emboldening those faced with persecution and death to remain firm in the faith;

3. the songs declared that power, wealth, and wisdom belong to the Lamb who was slain, thereby tacitly warning Christians not to let the prosperous times lull them into a state of spiritual torpor.

The strains of the heavenly music continue to be echoed in Christian worship today and its implications remain the same. The sounds are both assuring and unsettling:

1. Those who sing "Holy, holy, holy, Lord God Almighty" continue to confess a singular loyalty to God in the militant recognition that "Only thou art holy, there is none beside thee, Perfect in pow'r in love and purity."[28]

2. Hymns still voice the confident hope that "The saints who here in patience their cross and sufferings bore, shall live and reign forever when sorrow is no more. Around the throne of glory the Lamb they shall behold; in triumph cast before him their diadems of gold."[29]

3. The complacent, however, should be "startled at the solemn warning" implicit in this material, in order to prepare with renewed zeal to see "the Lamb, so long expected, come with pardon down from heav'n."[30]

---

27. Aune, "The Influence of Roman," 5–26.

28. From the hymn "Holy, Holy, Holy," Reginald Heber, 1783–1826.

29. From the hymn "Rejoice, Rejoice, Believers," Laurentius Laurentii, 1660–1722.

30. From the hymn "Hark! A Thrilling Voice Is Sounding," Anonymous; Koester, "The Distant Triumph Song," 237.

Songs Above the Spiral of Terror

The Lamb took the scroll, opened its seals, and thereby unleashed the kaleidoscopic visions of horror and splendor that dominate the central part of the book. The drama does not unfold in a straight line, but moves forward in a spiraling motion, in which readers are taken through successive cycles of tribulations, each culminating with a vision of divine glory.[31]

Interpreters have often tried to construct timelines based on the book of Revelation in the hope of finding some security in knowing how far we are from the end. But the spiraling cycles of visions make it impossible to place any confidence in our ability to discern the timing of the end, driving us back repeatedly to trust in God alone.

As the first four seals were broken,[32] the Four Horsemen came thundering forth to carry out their grisly tasks of conquest, war, famine, and death. At the fifth seal, the martyrs beneath God's heavenly altar cried out, "How long?" but were told to wait a little longer.[33] Earthquakes, darkness, and terror intensified with the opening of the sixth seal, until the peoples of the earth cried out that the great day of divine wrath had come, asking who could stand before it. As if in response, the scene shifts to the 144,000 sealed for God and to the great multitude that no one could number, dressed in radiant white before the throne, with palm branches in their hands, blessing God.[34] With the great tribulation now behind them, the question is asked:

> Who is this host arrayed in white,
> Like thousand snow-clad mountains bright,
> That stands with palms and sings its psalms,
> Before the throne of light?

And the response is given:

> These are the saints who kept God's Word;
> They are the honored of the Lord.
> He is their prince who drowned their sins,
> So they were cleansed, restored.[35]

---

31. Collins, Crisis and Catharsis, ix–xiv.

32. Rev 6.

33. The second verse of the hymn "All Hail the Power of Jesus' Name" (Edward Perronet, 1779) includes the martyrs who call from beneath the altar,

34. Rev 7.

35. Rev 7:13–17; Koester, "The Distant Triumph Song," 243–47.

The victorious scene helps to inspire the faith of readers still facing the prospect of suffering, knowing that God holds the future.

The blissful vision of the saints culminated with a great silence in heaven; this quickly gave way to another turbulent cycle of tribulations on earth as seven angels prepared to blow their trumpets. When the first four angels sounded a call, the earth was scorched and the sea turned to blood, a blazing star fell from heaven making the rivers bitter, and the lights in the heavens were darkened.[36] The sound of the fifth trumpet brought forth a plague of locusts from the bottomless pit that inflicted torment upon the faithless, and the sixth trumpet released millions of cavalry whose horses killed a third of humankind with the deadly fire and smoke issuing from their mouths.[37] Two of God's faithful witnesses were martyred and resurrected, the earth trembled, and the seventh angel sounded his trumpet as a chorus in heaven rang out:

> The kingdom of the world has become
> The kingdom of our Lord and of his Christ,
> And he shall reign forever and ever.[38]

The twenty-four elders bowed in worship and joined in celebrating the glorious reign of God. Yet readers are again swept away by another series of visions in which the kingdom of the world is emphatically not the kingdom of God and his Christ. First, there is a war in heaven and Michael's angelic hosts hurl Satan, in the form of a serpent, down upon the earth where he persecutes the woman who represents the people of God.[39] In the second and third visions, the power of Satan becomes incarnate in a beast that rises out of the sea to persecute the saints and in a beast that rises out of the land to constrain all people to idolatry.[40] The distant song of the saints on Mt. Zion drifts gently through the fourth vision, until a voice announces "the glory of the coming of the Lord" for judgment in the fifth vision, and an angel "trampled out the vintage where the grapes of wrath are stored," producing a river of blood that would surpass the carnage of any battlefield (Rev 14).[41] But again the cycle culminates with the saints beside the sea

36. Rev 8.

37. Rev 9.

38. Rev 11:15.

39. Rev 12.

40. Rev 13.

41. The imagery is incorporated into "The Battle Hymn of the Republic," Julia Ward Howe, 1861.

of glass, sharing in God's victory by remaining faithful to death. Like the Israelites who celebrated God's triumph over pharaoh beside the sea,[42] the saints sang the song of Moses,[43] which now became the song of the Lamb:

> Great and wonderful are thy deeds, O Lord God the Almighty!
> Just and true are thy ways, O King of the ages![44]

This celebration of deliverance is followed by another cycle of seven visions that recall the plagues visited on the Egyptians of old.[45] People were afflicted with sores, and waters were turned to blood; the sun's fiery heat scorched the land, the earth became engulfed in darkness; foul frog-like spirits assembled kings of the whole world for battle; and enormous hailstones fell from the sky. Then God made the great adversary of his people drink the cup of his wrath. This great antagonist has an almost timeless character. It is called "Babylon," after the city whose armies destroyed the first temple in 586 BC, yet it is portrayed as a city set on seven hills, like Rome, the city whose armies destroyed the second temple in AD 70. The city is also depicted as a harlot, which recalls the way the Scriptures depicted Israel's enemies of various times and places, including Nineveh[46] and Tyre.[47] The destruction of this foe is accompanied by a kind of dirge for the fallen city[48] followed by a resounding "Hallelujah chorus":

> Alleluia: for the Lord God omnipotent reigneth.[49]

The destruction of the harlot was complete; the bride had made herself ready, and the voices of a great multitude announced that the marriage supper of the Lamb had come. Or had it? Again, readers are hurled back into the fray, and the wedding feast has to wait for another thousand years. A rider on a white horse appears—not the menacing rider who appeared before in league with famine and death,[50] but Christ himself.[51] Now the

---

42. Exod 15:1–18; cf. Deut 32:1–43.

43. Exod 15:1–18; see chapter 1 of this book.

44. Rev 15:3.

45. Exod 7–11.

46. Nah 3:4.

47. Isa 23:17.

48. Rev 18.

49. Rev 19:6, KJV (used in "Hallelujah" from Handel's *Messiah*).

50. Rev 6:1–2.

51. Rev 19:11–21.

"Son of God goes forth to war a kingly crown to gain. His blood-red banner streams afar; who follows in his train?" What the hymn calls a "banner" is actually Christ's own robe, which is stained with blood before this battle begins, for this warrior is the Lamb, who triumphs through his own suffering and death. Those who follow in his train are the hosts of heaven arrayed in white, who witness Christ conquer by the power of his word. Satan is bound for a thousand years and the martyrs are raised to share Christ's blessed rule.

Afterward, Satan is released to meet his final doom. The dead are raised, the judgment is given,[52] and—at last—the New Jerusalem descends to be the bride of Christ.[53] Those who read the book of Revelation find themselves tumbling through cycle after cycle of visions, each culminating with a glimpse of divine glory that is often celebrated in song. This dizzying progression makes it impossible to fit the events portrayed here into a neat timeline. Readers can take no comfort in their own ability to discern the nearness of the end. The book does not enable us to determine whether we are living at the time of the sixth seal,[54] the fourth trumpet,[55] or the fifth plague.[56] The spiraling images of savagery and blessedness do permit us to declare that the evil we experience is real, but not final. The terrors may mount in cycle after cycle, threatening to become unbearable, but,

> when the strife is fierce, the warfare long, steals on the ear the distant triumph song, and hearts are brave again and arms are strong, Alleluia! Alleluia![57]

Songs of the New Jerusalem

The vision of the New Jerusalem has probably inspired more songs and hymns than any other portion of the book of Revelation. The promise that the sorrow and sufferings of this life will give way to endless bliss in a city paved with gold continues to capture the imaginations of Christian

52. Rev 20.

53. Rev 21:1–8.

54. Rev 6:12.

55. Rev 8:12.

56. Rev 16:10.

57. From the hymn "For All the Saints," William Walsham How, 1864; Koester, "The Distant Triumph Song," 246.

people—Mark Twain notwithstanding. The vision of the city has often been understood as a vivid expression of human aspirations. We lament, "Jerusalem, my happy home, when shall I come to thee? When shall my sorrows have an end? Thy joys when shall I see?" And in response we hear of the "happy harbor of the saints, O sweet and pleasant soil! In thee no sorrow may be found, no grief, no care, no toil."[58] But when we consider the New Jerusalem vision in its context in Revelation, it becomes apparent that to sing of the New Jerusalem is to sing of the faithfulness of God.

The descent of the city fulfills a chain of biblical promises. In Revelation 21:1–4 we see a new heaven and a new earth, and a joyous city, for the former things have passed away, as Isaiah foretold.[59] The New Jerusalem is adorned as a bride prepared for her husband,[60] and death is no more.[61] The city will be God's promised dwelling place, where he will be their God and they will be his people.[62] The echoes of biblical promises continue in Revelation 21:5–8, where God offers water to the thirsty[63] and grants everyone who is faithful the dignity of becoming his son.[64]

Even the features of the New Jerusalem confirm God's faithfulness to the promises. Long before, the prophet Ezekiel had been taken to a high mountain and shown a city that resembled a sanctuary; it was perfectly square and had twelve gates named for the twelve tribes of Israel.[65] The seer of Revelation watched as the city with its twelve gates descended from heaven, but in a splendor that surpassed anything presaged in the Old Testament.[66] Its walls were fifteen hundred miles long and fifteen hundred miles high—truly a "Jerusalem whose towers touch the skies."[67] The city was illuminated by the glory of God, as Ezekiel had promised, and living waters flowed through its streets around the tree of life, which bore its fruit

---

58. From the hymn "Jerusalem, My Happy Home," Josepeh Bromehead, 1795.

59. Isa 65:17–19.

60. Isa 61:10.

61. Isa 25:8.

62. Lev 26:11–12; Ezek 37:27; Zech 2:10–11.

63. Isa 55:1.

64. 2 Sam 7:14.

65. Ezek 40:1–4; 48:30–35.

66. Rev 21:9–21.

67. From the hymn "Jerusalem, Whose Towers Touch the Skies," Johannes Matthhaeus Meyfart, 1633.

all year.[68] In the context of the Scriptures as a whole, to sing, "Thy gardens and thy gallant walks continually are green; there grow such sweet and pleasant flow'rs as nowhere else are seen" is to confess that God's promises will not fail.

Revelation is fundamentally a book about God and the Lamb. In it, the end is not an event, but a person.[69] God is the Alpha and the Omega, the beginning and the end,[70] and the climactic vision in the book rings with the announcement that his "words are trustworthy and true."[71] The jewels of the city glisten brightly and its gardens are filled with luxuriant foliage, but the saints turn to the throne of God and the Lamb, worshipping God face to face.[72] The music displayed throughout this book certainly set an expectation for us of what heaven will be like. The hymns inspired by the book of Revelation work to the same end, seeking to capture singers for the Lord, so that

> From earth's wide bounds, from ocean's farthest coast,
> Through gates of pearl streams in the countless host,
> Singing to Father, Son, and Holy Ghost: Alleluia! Alleluia![73]

---

68. Ezek 43:1–5; 47:1–12; Rev 21:22—22:2.

69. Caird, *Commentary*, 155.

70. Rev 1:8; 21:6.

71. Rev 21:5; 22:6.

72. Rev 22:3–4; Koester, "The Distant Triumph Song," 243.

73. "For All the Saints," final verse; Koester, "The Distant Triumph Song," 242–56.

PART 2

Music in Worship: Heaven on Earth

Music is God's gift to man, the only art of heaven given to earth, and the only art of earth we take to heaven.

—WALTER SAVAGE LANDOR (1775–1864)

IN HEAVEN WE WILL be in a different body.[1] Consequently it is probable that music will be inconceivably different from our mortal experience. Even our imagination will be unable to comprehend the beautiful and incredible music of heaven. As evidenced in the previous chapters, the biblical foundation for training musicians and utilizing skilled musicians in the leading of corporate worship is a simple foundation for leading the church in music. In heaven, we will not be setting the standards—they will be set by the author of all creation. Until then, we must rely on the standards, set forth by Scripture, to guide our artistic efforts. When developing a philosophy of worship many factors must be considered. Pastors and musicians must strive to agree on a belief and how it is interpreted. We must work together to ensure the texts, music, and leadership for worship are consistent with the church doctrine and belief of its ministry strategy. The excerpt below is from the Philosophy of Music Ministry at Second Presbyterian Church, Memphis, Tennessee:

> We believe that congregational sung texts in the church should express, explicitly or implicitly, the glory of God in musical settings that are both beautiful and accessible to the people. We believe

1. 1 Cor 15:40.

that words sung should be theologically sound, spiritually helpful, aesthetically beautiful, culturally relevant, and liturgically appropriate, and that the musical texts should have musical integrity, artistic beauty, and liturgical usefulness. Our music should reflect the diversity of God's creation, just as our preaching consists of the whole counsel of God. We believe our musicians, liturgists and preachers should be faithful both to the truth of God and also to the creative beauty of God.

Truly, worship is a holy affair and by nature, transcends this world. In 1 Peter 2:9, we are reminded that "we are a chosen race, a royal priesthood, a holy nation, a people for God's own possession, so that you may proclaim the excellencies of him who has called you out of darkness into his marvelous light." So, to be holy, is to be set apart from the world—in order to reflect the true nature of God. As presented in what we know about New Testament worship, Paul teaches us in Romans 12:2, "do not be conformed to this world, but be transformed by the renewing of your mind." Most certainly our earthly worship of God should reflect a life transformed—far greater than what we experience in the flesh.

D. G. Hart and John Muether discuss this further in their book *With Reverence and Awe*. In fact, the section heading is called "Unapologetic Worship," which is an excellent reminder of the high calling God demands in our worship. The authors point out that the contrast between the world and the church should be most obvious when the church is at worship. The implication of worship practices being modeled by the world seems anticlimactic in a world filled with entertainment-driven mediums.

> "User-friendly" or "seeker-sensitive" worship is not an option for the people of God. In fact, worship that demonstrates the separateness of the church is what we could call merciful unkindness because it testifies to the world of the hope that is within us. If the world mocks us, so be it. True worship is for the church, not the world.[2]

2. Hart and Muether, *With Reverence and Awe*, 26.

CHAPTER 6

Choirs of Angels

When natural music is sharpened and polished by art, then one be-
gins to see with amazement the great and perfect wisdom of God in
his wonderful work of music, where one voice takes a simple part and
around it sing three, four, or five other voices, leaping, springing round
about, marvelously gracing the simple part, like a square dance in
heaven with friendly bows, embracings, and hearty swinging of the
partners. He who does not find this an inexpressible miracle of the
Lord is truly a clod and is not worthy to be considered a man.

—MARTIN LUTHER [1]

WE WILL MOVE FORWARD in our journey by identifying the common forms
of worship and music that is our common experience. We have identified
that there will be singing and playing of instruments, and that all of God's
children will be singing his praise. These chapters will attempt to advance
the thinking of basic church music to be what we will anticipate in heaven.

The old phrase, "to whom much is given, much is required," may be
a forgotten one in our modern age of church music. At a time in America
when large, dynamic churches are the norm, our resources for leading
church music seem to be in decline. The emphasis on fewer musicians with
amplification has overshadowed choirs and orchestras in the churches that
once embraced these forces. The Old Testament picture of thousands of
musicians leading worship is being replaced by the growing demand for

1. Lull and Russell, *Martin Luther*, 188.

bands and praise teams. Contributing to this decline is the diminishing confidence by the large amount of novice and amateur singers who once sang in choirs in contrast to the highly commercialized, glitzy, and polished approach to the pop music idiom. The fact that God made us in his image should be the greatest confidence booster for all who use their voices to sing. If the image of God is perfect, the voice he has given each human should be also, right? First Corinthians 15:40 says, "there are heavenly bodies and earthly bodies, but the glory of the heavenly is of one kind, and the glory of the earthly is of another." Though all God's children may not feel they have great singing capabilities on earth, they will in heaven. We should be bold in our singing until that great day. Our time of singing on earth really is our practice for heaven and the perfect voice we will then have.

But, let's look a bit further. The fact that the Holy Scriptures tell the followers of Christ to sing over 240 times is significant evidence that singing in worship is a non-negotiable act of our praise. With each human voice being created by God and these emphatic instructions throughout Scripture, the question is not: can everyone sing? *Everyone can sing*, at least that's what Brigham Young University professor of voice Clayne Robison says. Robison is working to diminish the belief only talented people can sing. "I do believe that everyone has a singing voice," Robison said.[2]

Perhaps the more pertinent question is—How do we enable our congregations to offer a more perfect praise in song? With the combination of all human beings given a voice for singing and the emphasis of singing throughout Scripture, we can be certain that this is an important matter for the church.

There are many cultural implications that have caused our "singing in church" to decline. We must work as church musicians to remedy the false cultural influence. The issues are obvious to most in the field of music:

- The decline in school music education. The cut in education budgets and substitute of pop music in schools has led to a drastic shift in training in school-aged students toward a basic understanding of singing.

- Perfectionism. The pop and media culture constantly displays music and singing by highly polished artists, making an average person feel as if he or she will never accomplish this status of singing. So why try?

2. Madsen, "Everyone Can Sing," para 3.

- Focus on individualism. This culture knows individual singers more than they recognize groups of singers. The notion of singing in a group or choir is overshadowed by the goal of being a singing "star."

- Amplification. The use of micing the singers or choirs lessens the expectation of the congregants, or average singer, to fully participate because the singing is being "carried" by the pros.

So, what are Christians to do with the decline of singing in our culture and therefore in our churches?

The church must lead—and teach people to sing. Though singing may not be a part of the world's culture, singing is very important in Christian living. Because singing is referenced more than 240 times in the Scriptures, the mandate is for all Christians must sing—not just the choir. This leads to an important part in understanding the role of music in worship. I often tell our new member classes that the *congregation* is the most important choir we have at our church. Though we have a dozen choirs in which all ages and abilities can participate, the congregation must be engaged in the corporate praise that is from the mouths of all his people.

How do we do this? One way is to develop leaders. Not just choir directors and worship leaders, but develop singing abilities among our congregations. With a decline in choir programs in our churches, we have likewise declined in developing the singing of the church. Again, from the Philosophy of Music Ministry at Second Presbyterian Church:

> Given the priority of worship, and therefore music, in the Church, we believe it is important to provide outstanding leadership for our people. We believe that our musical and liturgical leaders need to be mature believers with pastoral hearts. We must be led into worship by those who personally know our ultimate Leader, the Son of David, the "sweet singer of Israel." In order for our worship to be sincere, the hearts of our leaders must be sincerely worshipful. We believe that the choir is a group of worship leaders who 1) help us in our congregational singing and worship, 2) give us a reminder of the heavenly choir we shall one day hear, and 3) speak musically at times to the Lord on the congregation's behalf.

Choirs do help congregations in leading song, but they also hold a standard for corporate singing. The beauty of choirs in Christ's church is that we celebrate beauty in the anticipated perfection we will all have in heaven as we sing praise around his throne—all like the *voices of angels*.

Sing to him, sing praises to him; tell of all his wondrous works!

—PSALM 105:2

CHAPTER 7

Instruments for Worship

Praise the Lord!
Praise God in his sanctuary;
praise him in his mighty heavens!
Praise him for his mighty deeds;
praise him according to his excellent greatness!
Praise him with trumpet sound;
praise him with lute and harp!
Praise him with tambourine and dance;
praise him with strings and pipe!
Praise him with sounding cymbals;
praise him with loud clashing cymbals!
Let everything that has breath praise the Lord!
Praise the Lord!

—PSALM 150

CHRISTENDOM HAS DEBATED THE use of musical instruments for centuries. They were formally introduced into Christian worship in the ninth century. The Greek Orthodox churches still do not use instruments today. The Swiss Reformers reverted to the ancient practice of non-instrumental worship and were followed by the Scottish Presbyterians and English Puritans. American Presbyterians, Congregationalists, and Baptists began to use instruments around the beginning of the nineteenth century. The Scottish Presbyterians maintained the old ways until the 1850s.[1]

Building on the premise that it is permissible to use musical instruments in public worship, which ones ought to be used? The Psalms mention a whole range of string and wind instruments. Some of the instruments of the Old Testament may have been employed in connection with the sacrificial system. When the burnt offering began, the song of the Lord also began with the trumpets, accompanied by the instruments of David.[2] It may be that the instruments functioned to cover the sounds of animals being slaughtered, even as incense covered the stench. Be that as it may, the primary and normative use of instruments in our context of a service that is built on congregational participation is accompanying congregational singing. Instruments do not themselves praise; they accompany, support, and enrich the intelligent sung praise of the gathered congregation.

Accompanying the Congregation

Terry Johnson from Independent Presbyterian Church of Savannah, Georgia, addresses the issue of accompanying congregational singing very poignantly:

> Which of them do the best job of this? A variety of instruments may be permitted. Neither is the issue what might effectively accompany the singing of a choir, or of a soloist, or of a small group Bible study. The question is, which instrument(s) might most effectively accompany, support, and enrich the congregational singing of public worship? That would depend upon what people like, wouldn't it? Some will prefer one kind of instrument, others another. It's all a matter of taste, isn't it? As a matter of history and fact, personal or group preference has not been the method by which this question has been resolved. As a democratic society, we are accustomed to thinking in these terms. But majority preference misleads us on these and other questions. Instead, an ecclesiastical consensus was reached through a sense of what was suitable and appropriate. Popular or even folk instruments, prior to modern times, have never been considered suitable. The near universal verdict of Christendom through the centuries is that keyboard instruments are best for public worship: they best lead, they are best suited. The younger

1. Wilson-Dickson, *The Story of Christian Music*, 126.

2. 2 Chr 29:26–28.

generations often assume that this is just an arbitrary cultural preference. But this assumption is unproven and false. Tommy Dorsey and his band would be accompanying the singing in "traditional" churches if the older generation had tried to impose its musical preferences on the church in the way that younger ones have. The churches of Christendom house organs and pianos not because one generation prefers them, but because the verdict of many generations is that they are superior to all others for the specific purpose of supporting congregational singing.[3]

There are many options and combinations of instruments available for use in worship. We will not say what can or cannot be used here, but will simply encourage the church leaders to consider the most basic implication in choosing music for worship. It is not necessarily about what instruments are used, but how they are used. While beautiful instrumental music is an added dimension to many church services as preludes, postludes, and even meditations during the corporate worship, the case for careful consideration in the ultimate purpose of the musician in the service should be accompanying the singing of God's people. While a single guitar may be suitable to accompany a few people singing together at camp or in a home setting, a congregation of fifty or more people will need greater support and reinforcement to be able to sing confidently. Church musicians and pastors should plan accordingly to make sure the average congregant feels supported while singing in church. Terry Johnson raises more good questions for us:

> Which instrument will be 1) loud enough to effectively support and yet not overwhelm the singing; 2) sophisticated enough to distinctively sound each note; and 3) appropriate, as determined by its inherent qualities and associations? Guitars have become popular for public worship in recent years. We use them in our home Bible studies and in Sunday School. We use them at Point Pleasant before the start of our formal worship. For these uses they perform admirably. But we don't use them during the evening service itself, or even more to the point, we don't use them Sunday morning. Have we made arbitrary distinctions? Does our practice reflect what is merely a cultural bias? We don't think so. Why? Because for formal public worship guitars fail (or at least earn a weak grade) on all three tests. Respecting the first test, they are not loud enough once a meeting moves to a space that is larger than a living room (or once a larger room fills up). To make up for this guitarists, even multiple guitarists, will strum chords loudly,

3. Johnson, "Worship and Music Today," para 14.

but then the guitar fails the second test. Typically guitarists only play chords and don't play the melody at all, never mind all four parts. You may have noticed it is difficult to learn a tune when the melody is not being played. The medium then begins to impact the message, as "chords alone" playing typically requires simple and repetitious tunes. It is no accident that guitars and choruses go hand-in-hand. They are suited for each other. Only with great exertions can they be used to accompany the more complex tunes of traditional hymns and Psalms. Stringed instruments simply lack the versatility of keyboard instruments. Because the piano and organ combine melody, harmony, and rhythm, they provide better support for the singing of hymns in congregational settings.[4]

It is clear, that while a variety of instruments can be used for worship, and as the psalmist points out, the praise with a variety of instruments is prescribed in Holy Scriptures, we can now see the most practical implication for having instruments in worship, and that is accompanying the congregation in singing. And, the point here specifically is not against the guitar, but is an example of the considerations needed in use of instruments. Of course, with amplification, guitar and other similar instruments can be effective in tender moments of the worship service, but Johnson makes a valid point in what instruments better support a singing congregation.

When we observe the typical worship service in evangelical churches, the bulk of music in the liturgy is the singings of songs and hymns. Most modern liturgies with bands and praise teams embrace a paradigm of singing twenty to thirty minutes of praise music and the more formal liturgies will include numerous hymns and congregational responses. The majority of playing by church musicians in a given service is to accompany singing. This practically forms our makeup of what instruments will be used and even what musical arrangements may be used in worship. In our worship service, with an average of 1,000 people in attendance, we occasionally use a classical guitar for a prayer meditation. Even when amplified, the timbre of the guitar has not proven to be capable of carrying the entire congregation.

4. A recent favorable review of classical guitarist Paul Galbraith, in the *Wall Street Journal* describes his attempts to overcome the guitar's "limitations," which it says "have kept it a stepchild in classical circles." Noting one of its "traditional strengths" as "the sense of intimacy it imparts," it goes on to reason that this "inherent intimacy can be a weakness, making it harder to project the instrument in today's large concert halls." This is our first point exactly. Moreover, guitar performances, this otherwise positive review argues, "often lack the nuances of phrasing and interpretive depth" characteristic of other instruments. This is our second point (Jepson, "Turning the Guitar,").

I may have the guitar lead an introduction into a hymn or song, but we will add organ or piano when the congregation is to enter. Effective use of instruments can enhance worship and even provide a variety of textures, which is welcome in keeping our services fresh and creative.

Understanding the Organ

The presence of pipe organs (or any organ for that matter) has been historically most associated with the church. Surprisingly, the use of the pipe organ in American churches is more widespread than popular commentary recognizes. In fact, the American Guild of Organists reported in 2011 an increase in new organs built over the past ten years from that of the previous twenty years from many of its members.[5] Here, the purpose is to inform and educate on some of the ideas and reasons organs have historically been in churches in America.

Organs became a part of most churches in the United States regularly in the early to mid 1800s. For many historic churches in America, the sustainability of the pipe organ has been questioned. With the development of new musical forms, organ music has been less familiar than it was with the rise of new churches in America and the interest in classical music by many of our country's newfound wealthy to model after the major European cities and cathedrals.

In a very scholarly study of church architecture in America, Jeanne Kilde, in her book *When Church Became Theatre*, speaks of the initial purpose of organs and then its changing roles throughout the nineteenth century.

> The first organs made their appearance in American Congregational churches in the 1770's and 1780's. Integrated initially as an aid to congregational singing, instruments and choirs quickly moved to anthem performances sans congregation.
>
> The growing use of organs also led to a shift in the spatial arrangements. When first introduced, organs and other instruments were located within the gallery opposite the pulpit,[6] and congregants stood and faced the back of the room during musical pieces. Early nineteenth century revivalism, however, relocated the organ

---

5. Swan, "The Presidents Report," 3.
6. Following European tradition.

and choir to the preaching platform and eliminated the earlier awkward practice.[7]

By the time many of the great churches were built in America, the pipe organ was the far more devolved instrument that could produce enough sound to support the congregational singing and to also play more than just a single melody with only one musician needed. It is also important to note the association of organs in America during the two periods we now classify as "The Industrial Age," which was preceded and followed by parts of "The Great Awakening Movement." These combined movements produced many churches throughout our country and a vast amount of wealth. Kilde goes on to talk about the trend in church architecture in the 1860s, during which the placement of pipe organs becomes central and quite impressive.

> Amphitheatre audience rooms shared a number of characteristic features. Almost invariably, an elevated choir loft or alcove occupied the rear stage wall, and above it dramatically rose a large case of organ pipes.[8]

Kilde later offers some motivation behind the architecture, artistry, and symbolism of the organ in Protestant churches of the same era.

> The most prominent element accommodated by the evangelical pulpit stage . . . was the organ. Positioned against the front wall of the church, above and behind both pulpit and choir loft, the huge bank of organ pipes sored to the ceiling of auditorium sanctuaries. Congregations boasting of the "largest," "finest," "most musical" organs in the land wanted them placed in full view of visitors. Intricately stenciled, elaborately encased, or arranged in a solid screen, or "pipe fence," organ pipes lent both an aural and visual richness to the worship experience. The more common front-and-center placement of the organ . . . visually indicated the central importance of the organ as the quintessential ecclesiastical instrument. With pipes that might reach 16 feet high, the instrument suggested something of the awe of the Gothic verticality that often featured classical detailing.[9]

The presence of pipe organs in most American sanctuaries during the nineteenth century certainly developed a rich musical culture within churches. This, in turn, developed many fine musicians—organists and

7. Kilde, *When Church Became Theatre*, 45.

8. Ibid., 77.

9. Ibid., 12–24.

choirs alike. The association of the organ with the church was not only musical, but was representative of the visual grandeur the organ brought to churches. The use of organs not only displayed the wealth and commitment required to build such great instruments but followed the model of presenting fine and grand houses of worship, similar to the European cathedrals, for the worship of God. Many books on the development of Gothic cathedrals parallel the desire for great churches with the Old Testament temple and the basic human desire to build temples and to create things in the image of God (*imago Dei*).[10] The church, or temple, was often thought to offer a "little heaven on earth." It is evident in the building of most of America's churches, that the pipe organ was a common way of creating *majesty* and *grandeur* within the sanctuary. The musical scale and diversity that the pipe organ represents in church worship can be paralleled with the mass musical feast in which we expect to participate while in heaven.

For additional consideration, again, Terry Johnson makes a great point regarding what musical genres instruments are often associated, and how the organ has a unique place in the church service.

> The third point raises the problem of associations. A saxophone suffers from its association with the nightclub scene. Banjos suffer from association with square dances and Hee Haw. Guitars suffer from two associations: the first is the casual setting of the campfire and other informal occasions for which it is so famously known and loved, which, however, undermine its suitability for transcendent public worship. This problem might become clearer when we consider harmonicas and kazoos, which are clearly or comically inappropriate. Could we use a harmonica to accompany our congregational singing? We could. It wouldn't be unscriptural, in the sense that there is no Bible verse that forbids it. But would it be appropriate? Obviously it wouldn't. Not only does it do a poor job of supporting the singing, but it lacks dignity. In a crisis it could be pressed into service. But normally we would seek a more sophisticated and versatile instrument. But back to the guitar. Richard Brookhiser has called it "the ultimate E-Z-2-Play instrument." He asks, "why else was it the lyre of the American peasantry?" The relative ease with which it can be learned to play (say, as compared with the violin), has placed it prominently in the midst of popular and informal settings. This informality is an obstacle to be overcome for those who wish to cultivate an atmosphere of solemn reverence in the public worship of our great God.[11]

10. See chapter 13.

11. Johnson, "Worship and Music Today," para 16.

It is no question that we associate instruments with certain genres of music. In my own experience as a church organist, I've heard testimony of people who associate the sounds of the organ with being in church. It has been a common connection in Western churches for well over 500 years. The origins of the pipe organ are rooted in the church and the ability of these instruments to produce a variety of volumes, timbres, voices, and overall sounds is unparalleled. It is for these simple and practical reasons that pipe organs have been used in churches for so long.

However, this has not always been the case. "The organ was, for a long time, not used to accompany congregational singing, but had its own voice, of equal status to and independent of the singers. The objections to organ music which led to the Calvinists stripping the Genevan churches of their organs were therefore nothing to do with the organ's secular associations. Rather, it was the 'popish' habit of taking away from the congregation words which were rightly theirs to utter."[12] The organ has many merits and benefits for church use. The sustaining quality, as well as the tone of the organ allow maximum support for accompanying voices. The wide range of the instrument can simultaneously offer low, middle, and high range contributions while only be played by a single musician. The pipe organ is the most common and frequently used instrument that can provide the colors and contrast of an orchestra of any size. Further, the combination of organ with orchestra or any other instrument or ensembles can offer maximum diversity in musical expression and accompaniment for congregation as well as without. The organ alone, or with instruments, is synonymous with church music, and has been so for many centuries.

While there is certainly no requirement for any church to have an organ, it is important for both those who favor the organ, and those who do not, to at least understand its place in the history of church, particularly the short history of the American church. It is important before throwing out such massive and costly instruments that the church think about its musical and architectural contributions, its association and opportunity to counter worldly music, and its ability to ably lead in the corporate expression of song. It is perhaps, also, an opportunity to display qualities of God and the great heaven he has in store for us—to revel in the unique sounds that could transport our souls, hearts and minds while on earth to the heavenly sanctuary of God himself.

12. Wilson-Dickson, *The Story of Christian Music*, 77–78.

CHAPTER 8

Corporate Worship Music

As WE HAVE IDENTIFIED the role of choirs and instruments in heaven, we must now address the most important aspect of church music—congregational singing and participation. As mentioned earlier, I often tell our choirs and congregation that even amidst these, the fine musical ensembles of choirs in our music ministry, the most important choir is the congregation. It is important that churches, even ones with very good choirs or other professional singers, encourage the importance of corporate singing together in church. Brian Wren has devoted an entire book on this matter, and the title alone—*Praying Twice: The Music and Words of Congregational Song*—says much.

> Charles Wesley invited sailors and Methodists to 'rescue the holy pleasure'[1] of singing together. In eighteenth-century England, communal song was a normal part of everyday life. Wesley needed to rescue, not the act of singing together, but the 'innocent sound' of Christian song.[2]

A very important aspect of creating opportunity for corporate singing is how we view corporate singing. Wren goes on to describe congregational song as,

> Anything sung by a group of people assembled to worship God, not as a presentation to some other group, but as a vehicle for their

---

1. Part of the lyric written in Plymouth, 1746. For text and anecdote see Young, *Music of the Heart*, 170.

2. Wren, *Praying Twice*, 47.

worship. The content, musical style, and liturgical function of such songs can be quite varied, but if it is group singing, community singing, it is congregational song.

We have pointed out the shifts in the quality of songs used in churches and how some of these changes have made corporate participation more challenging. We have lived through a period when personal preference has become the principal factor in determining the music we choose for worship. Our heavenly perspective of music should tell us that what we do now is look to the future of our heavenly music. However, there is a danger in looking at what we do now without a heavenly perspective. We must keep in mind that there are excellent things happening in church music now.

There is wonderful new hymnody being written and inspired that is working well in all musical settings of church music. Perhaps this is reclamation of criteria for songs well suited for corporate worship—no matter the age of the song, the setting of the worship, the songs that have both musical and textual integrity will work in all situations.

Teaching Corporate Worship Music

Because of our culture's unlimited access to recorded music, people can hear music, especially new music, whenever they want. We can also select our preferred stations and create playlists of our favorite music. It could be that this phenomenon has also given the church an indication of how we teach new music to our congregations. In the contemporary realm of music, we could assume that when we introduce a new song in corporate worship, many people have already heard it and already know or are at least familiar with it. Certainly for popular Christian music that is recorded and widely dispersed, this is helpful. But, how do we teach the great hymns, psalms, and spiritual songs that are beyond the contemporary music realm?

In an article entitled "Sing a New Song: But Why?" written to our congregation in the monthly newsletter, I raised some points for them that I propose all church leaders, especially pastors and church musicians, consider when planning congregational singing.

> Those of us who are involved in worship planning often hear comments like, "I didn't recognize that last hymn" or "We didn't sound too good on that one." If you have entertained similar thoughts yourself, you are not alone. Worship is most certainly a time when we want to feel free to openly sing our praises and supplications to

God, and knowing the song or hymn makes this easier and more natural. When we plan worship, we want to incorporate hymns that we are confident our congregation knows well. So rest assured, week to week, we are wrestling with the same questions.

How do we determine what hymns or songs are best known by all? This is an important question to address because selecting hymns can be a tricky process. When a church congregation is comprised of multiple denominational backgrounds, new Christians, and mature Christians, it's easy to see why some are more familiar with some hymns than with others. The *Trinity Hymnal* alone has more than 700 hymns, excluding many from churches past and adding countless new and excellent songs being written today. In 1997, our church appointed a committee to evaluate our use of the *Trinity Hymnal*. The study revealed that our congregation knew 160 hymns from the hymnal. At that time, an additional eighty-three hymns were identified as important to learn, and twenty-seven were thought to be especially useful. Since that initial study years ago, our congregation has sung 248 different hymns in our worship services. Of those 248 hymns, we feel confident that our congregation can sing 206 of these with ease. In sixteen years our church has collectively learned forty-six new hymns, excluding any hymns not printed in the *Trinity Hymnal*. This is a formidable accomplishment for any congregation!

In 1964, church music scholar and author Eric Routley lamented over the fact that the average congregation only knew approximately 200 hymns. A relatively low number, when you consider that merely one hundred years ago, hymnals contained 800 to 1,200 selections—when you think about the output of hymns just from writers like Isaac Watts (approx. 600), Fanny Crosby (more than 8,000), and Charles Wesley (8,989 hymns), 1,200 hymns seems to be a fairly basic number; and this number does not include the 150 psalms! Because Scripture teaches us to sing "psalms, hymns, and spiritual songs," we can all agree that we have a great challenge before us in seeking to expand our scope and breadth of the many great songs available to us.

Should the church today lament the decline in common Christian hymnody that we use in worship? Let's compare some numbers. A 2008 study in London revealed that the average teen between the ages of eighteen and twenty-four, had illegally downloaded an average of 842 songs to his/her listening device. Presently, the average 16 gb-iPhone 5 can hold approximately 4,000 songs, each song averaging four minutes. Interestingly enough, further studies have shown that the average person uses half the capacity of his/her device to carry music. With that many people listening to around 2,000 songs on their phones or MP3 devices, I am challenged to think that the church can easily learn more hymns, psalms and spiritual songs. But why should we?

Psalm 33:3 says, "Sing to him a new song." The ESV Study Bible says, "new song need not imply a freshly composed song; instead it may mean singing a song as a response to a fresh experience of God's grace." Walter Brueggemann notes in his commentary that a "new song is one that sings about a new world . . . and to such a world the only appropriate response is confident and sure praise to the One who makes that world available to us."[3] It is clear that when we sing, it is God who gives us the melody of song in our hearts to sing and that as we grow in his grace, we are also brought to new and fresh understanding of his will. One of the benefits of singing is that we instill Scripture and theology into our hearts and minds with the repetition of the texts and words. As the melodies ring in our ears they remind us of these words in a very poignant way. As Brian Wren's title to his book on congregational singing suggests, we are literally *Praying Twice*. Why wouldn't we want to respond to God's grace in fresh new ways?

How do we learn new hymns and songs as a congregation? In worship. Christians who seek continued growth and discipleship in their lives should be open to the new songs that God puts in our path. Worship is a time of praising God and learning more from His word and songs can aid us in that effort. We as worship leaders seek to introduce new hymns and songs that we feel have great merit and have words and melodies that will be passed from generation to generation. As we look to the future and decide what hymns and songs to utilize in worship, we hope to teach hymns that may be unfamiliar to you. We pray that you will be receptive to the prospect of joining in the chorus and learning along side us. Please be assured that we thoughtfully plan new songs intermittently and prepare our choirs and musicians to lead the way for us to be successful. We believe that learning is enhanced by repetitiously immersing ourselves into the song. Wouldn't it be wonderful to look back in twenty years and marvel at the new songs God had put in our midst as a congregation? We have a great capacity for learning more songs and a vast repertoire of wonderful new mercies awaits us. Many historians regularly tout the role of hymns as a source of providing Christian doctrine, nurture, and reassurance. As Erik Routley simply states, "The duty of a hymn is to get the best out of people . . . so they can respond to

3. Brueggemann, *The Message of the Psalms*, 106.

what the Lord has done." May this be our collective mission as we sing a new song!

The congregation certainly is the most important choir. I was astonished one recent Sunday when the choir did not sing in that particular service. Just listening to the congregation sing "All Hail the Power of Jesus' Name" was a thrilling joy. This was an awesome picture of the congregation being the choir and the power of experiencing heaven through singing with all the saints and angels!

Implications for the Church:
Psalms, Hymns, and Spiritual Songs

Let the word Christ dwell in you richly, teaching and admonishing one another in all wisdom, singing psalms, hymns, and spiritual songs, with thankfulness in your hearts to God.

—COLOSSIANS 3:16

Hymns do not create truth, nor even reveal it; they celebrate it. They are the response of the trusting heart to a truth revealed or a fact accomplished. God does it and man sings it. God speaks and a hymn is the musical echo of His voice.

—A. W. TOZER[4]

. . . be filled with the Spirit, addressing one another in psalms, hymns, and spiritual songs, sing and making melody to the Lord with all your heart . . .

—EPHESIANS 5:18–19

Ephesians 5:19 and Colossians 3:16 both are clear that we are to sing psalms, hymns, and spiritual songs in praise to God. Paul goes on to say that corporate worship has a function of teaching and admonishing through the lyrics

---

4. Tozer, *Tozer on Worship*, 115.

of its songs, a very important aspect of communication in the oral culture of Paul's day.

I fear there is a misunderstanding in modern American evangelical interpretation to take this to mean something like psalms (from the book of the Bible), hymns (roughly, older style Christian songs), and modern Christian songs, which is an anachronistic approach to these words.

The original Greek phrase appears in both Colossians 3:16 and Ephesians 5:19 the same: *psalmois, humnois, kai odais pneumatikais*. Here is a brief explanation of these Greek words:

> psalmois—which means song, or *mizmor*, also meaning song, is used 920 times in the lexicon but mostly in the title lines of psalms (also the title lines of the Songs of Solomon). In Job 21:12 and 30:31, it refers to flute songs. In Amos 5:23, it translates as "music." In Zechariah 6:14, its phrase is not in the Hebrew. Isaiah 66:20 "with psalms" actually translates "in clean vessels."
>
> humnois—*tehillah*, a song of praise, thanksgiving, or adoration to God is found 32 times in the lexicon; 16 of those are in books that are not in the Protestant Bibles.
>
> odais pneumatikais—*odais* is simply a word for songs (so is, *shîr*, the Hebrew it translates). Pneumatikais means spiritual.[5]

It is also unclear if there is any appreciable difference between mizmor—"a psalm"—and shîr—"a song." Rabbinic interpretation recognizes *mizmœr* as a psalm accompanied by instruments and *shîr mizmœr* as a psalm sung by a choral group alone. Several things are clear, however, in relating these two words. One is that the noun *mizmœr* appears exclusively in the Psalms and always as a title and never in the body of a psalm. By contrast, shîr is not confined to the Psalter and within the Psalter itself is used both as a title and in the psalm proper. Second, although *mizmœr* as a noun is limited to psalm superscriptions the verbal form, it is most often used to mean a song.[6]

A third observation to be made is that *mizmœr* is limited to religious song. Shîr, on the other hand, may occasionally refer to secular songs. Isaiah 23:16 refers to the songs of the harlot (prostitute). Amos 8:10 would

---

5. *Strong's Exhaustive Concordance*; Wilson-Dickson, *The Story of Christian Music*, 234.

6. Brueggemann, *Spirituality of the Psalms*, 11.

indicate that religious songs can be turned into lamentations just as feasts can be turned into funerals.

It is no accident that the hymn and the lament are the two leading types of psalms in the Psalter, both illustrating two ways of addressing God: praise and petition. In one way the hymn is an expansion of the lament. To illustrate, Psalm 57 begins as a lament: "Have pity on me God . . . I take shelter in the shadow of your wings until the destroying storm is over . . . I lie surrounded by lions." By verse 7, however, the psalmist says, "My heart is steadfast, I will sing and make melody." The abrupt change of mood is obvious. Thus, most of the laments evolve into songs of praise in anticipation of God's deliverance. The Hebrew could always sing to his God in spite of forbidding circumstances.

> The hymn and the song of thanksgiving praise God and sing to God not in anticipation for an expected deliverance but in response to something already experienced. And even here there is a distinction. One, the hymn, praises God for his actions or extols him for who he is (descriptive praise: God is . . . God does . . .). The song of thanksgiving praises God for a specific deed (declarative praise: God has . . .).[7]

With these three words, Paul is telling us to sing songs with instruments, and *a cappella*, both about who God is (e.g., "How Great Thou Art") and what he has done (e.g., "Amazing Grace"), and that God accepts both praise and lament as they come from the heart of the believer.

This is an example of how we can think about biblical implications for heavenly worship thereby moving us beyond the imperfections of our own interpretations. Singing *psalms, hymns,* and *spiritual songs* is not a biblical mandate to sing different types of music in the twenty-first century. It is a reminder to both praise God, and to give him our petitions, and lament— and to do so with an eager expectation of redemption and deliverance.

The Role of Music in Liturgy

In corporate worship services, the music plays an integral part of the order of worship, or the liturgy. As we have already seen in Isaiah 6, and as Robert Webber has so eloquently impacted our worship leadership over the past many years, the dialogue of worship between God and his people is the

---

7. Westermann, *Blessing in the Bible*, 31.

essence of worship. The dialogue certainly echoes the pictures of the angels in Isaiah's dream crying "holy, holy, holy" back and forth and the way God responds to the praises with affirmation, confession with assurance, and blessings with a call to serve.

Webber believes there is a fourfold pattern in biblical worship: Assembling, Word, Eucharist, and Sending. Each of these acts is an enactment of the story of God, which we are called to embody. Within the worship model there are three things to consider as we assemble (called), listen and respond, give thanks, and enact social justice: content, structure, and style.

> Content is the most important part of worship. Worship is directed toward God and is about God. Losing either of these elements makes worship shallow and egocentric. Worship is a holistic life of obedience. Worship is also the Gospel at work in the world. It is the power of redemption experienced in the lives of the community of God. It is not simply ascribing "worth" to God, nor is it a message to the congregants. Worship is initiated by God and for God. That should sober our attempts at making worship relevant to us . . . especially since worship is not about us. Structure is a necessary and important part of worship. Every church has a structure which correlates with its view of worship. If we desire a more holistic worship experience, it is necessary to structure our worship to facilitate this desire. Content helps dictate the structure. In all things, our structures must participate in the "narrative" of God's story and not simply be a "presentation." Structure moves us from observers to participants in the grand narrative of the Gospel.[8]

This narrative in which we are privileged to participate is with all the saints and angels of heaven, and our worship on earth is part of this dialogical narrative. However, in heaven, with our perfect minds, bodies, and voices, our praises will be rolling off our tongues naturally. The songs of praise we sing will be "unceasing," as Scripture has taught us. The intent of liturgy reveals our human need for form. Dr. Old says,

> There are good reasons for having an established liturgy, and those reasons have often been recounted. In the first place, liturgical forms are a good means of teaching the essentials of the Christian faith. When familiar liturgical forms and texts are used again and again, it gives opportunity to meditate on them and to penetrate their meaning more deeply. When there are well-established

8. Webber, *Worship Old and New*, 23.

procedures with which everyone is familiar, it makes it easier to concentrate on the content rather than the outward form. Any athlete understands the importance of mastering form. Such simple things as breathing must be done correctly. It takes a long time to get some of these simple techniques down, but this is essential so that eventually they can be done spontaneously, without effort, without thinking of them. The concentration must be on other things. Forms are a means to an end; if they are constantly changing, they obscure the end rather than lead to it.[9]

There is a growing awareness of liturgy and the dialogical nature of God's speaking and our responding. Music is certainly an important part of the heavenly dialogue that takes place in those churches who recognize this format of worship. Terry Johnson observes the shift in corporate worship practices:

> Since the original publication of *Leading in Worship*, we can speak of the emergence of a third liturgical movement. The first two are well established. The "liturgical renewal movement" is influential among Roman Catholics and mainline Protestants, and has resulted in a convergence of liturgical practices within those groups. The highly-visible, semi-charismatic, seeker-friendly, and youth-oriented contemporary worship movement, with its popular worship music, is seemingly everywhere triumphant, with it ubiquitous praise bands, gregarious "worship leaders," opening 20-minute song sets, raised hands, casual tone, skits, and maybe even dance, and "relevant" sermons.
>
> Yet we can now speak of a third movement, which aims to restore traditional or historic Protestant worship. More specifically, for our purposes, we are interested in the growing momentum behind the revival of historical Reformed worship. Discouraged by the wrong turns represented by liturgical renewal *and* contemporary worship movements, dismayed by the widespread ignorance of the ministry and worship of the Reformed tradition within today's Presbyterian and Reformed churches, and disheartened by the abandonment of its biblically based and historically proven liturgical practices, growing numbers of theologians, pastors, and laymen have sought to restore Reformed churches to their Reformed liturgical heritage.[10]

9. Old, *Worship*, 165.

10. Johnson, *Leading in Worship*, v.

Gary Furr and Milburn Price, in their book, *The Dialogue of Worship*, summarize the important aspects of a dialogical form of liturgy with eight points:

1. God is the focus of the conversations of dialogic worship.

2. In dialogic worship, the worshippers are active (and interactive) participants.

3. In dialogic worship, the Word of God may be encountered through a variety of "messengers."

4. Dialogic worship includes and touches the relationships of human participants with one another as well as their relationship to God.

5. Dialogic worship implies a conversation between the content and tradition of the historic faith and the contemporary gathering of worshippers.

6. The primary functions of music are to facilitate the dialogue and to contribute to that dialogue.

7. Structures for worship services should embody the dialogic principles.

8. Worship is a conversation that is relevant to and connects with all dimensions of life.[11]

Understanding where a church's worship format has effect on planning and implementing music into the service is certainly of importance. The identity of a church's worship will most likely fall into one of the three broad categories of which Terry Johnson speaks. Heavenly worship will certainly be a dialogue in the presence of our God. Our Father will be in our presence and we will worship him with song and praises in response to the words from his tongue. That alone is reason to now begin practicing our posture of responding to him in heaven.

Characteristics of Good Congregational Song

John Calvin in his preface to the Geneva Psalter says

> As for public prayers, there are two kinds. The ones with the word alone: the others with singing . . . we know by experience that singing has great force and vigor to move and inflame the

11. Furr and Price, *the Dialogue of Worship*, conc.

hearts of men to invoke and praise God with a more vehement and ardent zeal. Care must always be taken that the song be neither light nor frivolous; but that it have weight and majesty (as St. Augustine says), and also, there is a great difference between music which one makes to entertain men at table and in their houses, and the Psalms which are sung in the Church in the presence of God and his angels.[12]

The center of a good ministry of music is based on the belief that the whole congregation is the most important singing body or choir we have. Though we strive to develop the gifts of especially talented individuals, and we believe allowing those to use their gifts in presenting the gospel through music is important, we want all present to offer praise through their lips in singing.

Regardless of culture or circumstance, God still demands us to sing praise to him. We feel it is the responsibility of the church, particularly the church musicians and pastors, to ensure that singing together as a body remains true to the mandates given in Scripture. Psalm 33:3b says "play skillfully and sing for joy." We should always present to God our most excellent offering. "I will bring nothing before the Lord which has cost me nothing."[13] Equally, the church hymnody has been rooted with strong musical and textual standards. It is our hope that the songs we sing reflect our desire for musical excellence and integrity, and that because of that, we hope they will enable God's people to sing boldly and confidently each week.

As we aim to offer God our best, we must be mindful that it is our job to equip the congregation to be successful in making a solid contribution to congregational song. There are many factors that help the average, nontrained singer to feel unrestrained while singing in church. Here we will address the practical goals of singing and what songs will help us towards those goals, what criteria make a good song, and the character of a song appropriate for a church congregation. These are the criteria we use in selecting appropriate music for our church services.

Goals of Congregational Singing

1. To encourage participation. The time of singing we offer in our worship is one of the main ways we engage our congregation in physically

12. Calvin, *Geneva Psalter*, i.

13. Ps 33:3.

and actively participating. We should make this is as familiar as possible and supply them with all they need to be successful: words large enough, printed melody, stable accompaniment, and all the needed musical requirements listed below to promote confidence.

2. To engage in worship. We want the people to be comfortable singing. The goal is to engage them in active worship and to be engaged in active worship. People must be comfortable and at ease. The more complications we throw at them, the more opportunity we allow for distraction and focus on earthly issues, rather than on God and his worship.

3. To teach gospel truths and Scripture. Some of the best songs are the ones that teach us Scripture and great attributes of the faith that stay with us throughout our lives. The Reformers of the church generally love the songs that are deep in theology and teaching.

4. To be intergenerational. Our worship involves all ages and nationalities, and therefore involves many cultural backgrounds and preferences. The idea of intergenerational worship is one that brings us all together, not alienating one generation or another and not catering to one preference or another. However, we should aim to promote unity throughout worship. This is one of the strengths of our current hymnody and use of hymns written from the fourth century to the present.

5. To be a testimony of the living church. The songs we sing are a vital affirmation of faith to those around us. Singing should be bold and confident and the songs we sing should enable us to confidently express our belief.

Characteristics of Song Well Suited
for the Typical Congregant

Church leaders, especially those selecting the actual songs to be sung by all, must understand the capability of the individual abilities of those in the pews for each corporate worship gathering.

We must consider the past musical training of the *average* worshipper in our churches. Though most arts advocates mourn the decline of music education in our schools, the church must still view the importance of training the whole church in singing. We could think of the congregation as ongoing "general music" class. The value is not for the individual's gain of musical knowledge, but of being better equipped to develop their skills as a worshipper. As church musicians, we must always know our congregation's limits and basic abilities for comprehending and being able to express the corporate music we expect them to embrace.

These are standards that can help guide a church musician or pastor in selecting hymns and songs with musical criteria that will serve a general audience of the average congregant:

1. Moderate vocal range. In today's culture, studies have shown that most people's vocal range is not as high as it was many years ago. Most people will feel comfortable with C as the bottom of the range and an E-flat as the top. This range is a bit over an octave, and is a safe place to engage most everyone.

2. Simple and stable rhythms. Most people know what a quarter note and a half note look like and what they mean. Eighth notes should be used sparingly and usually not with more than three or four together. Syncopated rhythms and long periods of rest usually cause insecurity and should be avoided. Complicated pick-up rhythms will sometimes cause entrances to be unsure.

3. Strong and memorable melody. A strong melody will have a notable climax and shape. It will move in a way that feels at ease, is easily repeated, and is memorable.

4. The ability to be sung confidently. Musical factors mostly determine this. The songs must suit themselves to be well accompanied by organ/ or piano, or any of the instruments that are most capable of supporting a large group of singers.

Characteristics and Mechanics of a Well-Crafted Song

Throughout the previous chapters we have discussed the characteristics of music appropriate for corporate worship based on biblical foundations and the general nature of its content and makeup.

1. Textual/syllabic accent. The songs that feel natural to the voice will align properly with the text. The syllabic stress will be aligned with the meter of the tune and fit the phrasing of the music. A well-crafted

song for singing will have a musical shape that fits the text and will naturally draw you to the words, not the music.

2. Harmonic structure. A good harmonic foundation usually supports an interesting and singable melody. The structure should have a natural progression. Songs with good harmonic structure support the rhythmic foundation and help people anticipate where the music is going. A harmony that moves at regular intervals gives more support than one that stays stagnant for long periods of time. Most good hymns have a harmonic structure that provides solid rhythm and supports the melody and the text.

3. Musical expression and climax. The songs that seem to last are the ones that not only have great texts, but also have a melody that expresses the sentiment of the text. Good tunes have a memorable shape, and the shape fits the text. The music should support the climax of the text, and the tune will intentionally move toward and/or come down from a climax. Music that speaks to our hearts will be expressive, well-shaped, and will have a natural musical phrase.

CHAPTER 9

Music on Earth

*Now among the other things proper to recreate man and give him
pleasure, music is either the first or one of the principal, and we must
think that it is a gift of God deputed to that purpose.*

—JOHN CALVIN [1]

AS MUSIC HAS DEVELOPED, so has the output, diversity, the array of genres,
and the love of music by people. One of the current differences is that fewer
people are making music than in past generations. We see this from the
declined enrollment and participation in church and school choirs. People
enjoy *listening* to music—not necessarily making music. The other issue is
the performance and perfection of music—the perfection of professional
musical artists deter our participation in music-making because of the
expectation that flashy performances have set. These issues have changed
how people perceive music, both at church and in general, but especially
at church. Here, we will look briefly at a few of the ways in which music
impacts faith and how the secular world looks at music in the church.

Faith and Music

Music has unexplainable power to influence faith. There are countless past
and current artists and performers who have used their faith in secular con-
texts and, in doing so, have demonstrated how artists can live a Christian life

1. Calvin, *Genevan Psalter*, preface.

within the context of their giftedness. My particular fascination on this front is with the great composer Johann Sebastian Bach. I, first, am fascinated with his simple life and faith—a man who, according to a recent *New York Times* article, is the greatest musical composer to have ever lived.[2] It is interesting that of all the musical giants we could name, the one with the highest musical output was for the use of the church in worship of God—is at the top. I personally consider J. S. Bach to be the "patriarch of church music." His influence of combining great music inspired by God, with his known faith, is still being used on earth to transport us to heaven. Even almost 300 years after his death, his music is still celebrated throughout the world.

Secondly, I am amazed with the power of his music and its unknowing effect on the secular populace. I observed this phenomenon firsthand while participating in a prominent music festival that is named for, and focuses on, the music of Bach. The performance was of the masterful oratorio *St. Matthew Passion*. Though sung in German, it had the English translation projected over the stage in the form of subtitles. The words, which clearly speak of Christ's life and death and the redemptive work he has done for humanity, are highly expressive and emotive of the Christian faith. Being that this performance was in a notoriously non-Christian part of the country, I was amazed at how passionately this music was celebrated obviously for its musical merit. Nonetheless, seeing the faith message being celebrated in a secular context was a powerful commentary for communicating the faith message through music.

Bach was virtually unknown as a composer, at least outside of the German towns where he quietly lived and worked. He was never attracted to stardom, fame, or fortune. This unquestionable genius was refreshingly modest and unassuming. He told a student, "Just practice diligently, and it will go very well. You have five fingers on each hand just as healthy as mine." And once, when an acquaintance praised Bach's wonderful skill as an organist, Bach replied, "There is nothing very wonderful about it; you have only to hit the right notes at the right moment and the instrument does the rest."[3]

Bach also said, "Music's only purpose should be the glory of God and the recreation of the human spirit."[4] Music was given to glorify God in heaven and to edify men and women on earth. It wasn't to make lots

2. Tommasini, "The Greatest," para. 2.

3. Gardiner, *Bach*, 178.

4. Ibid., 156.

of money, or to feed the musician's ego, or to be famous. Music was about blessing the Lord and blessing others. Most of his manuscripts were inscribed at the end with the initials SDG, *Soli Deo Gloria*, which translates "to God alone the glory."

Bach faithfully lived out these beliefs. Though he possessed a musical genius found perhaps once in a century, he chose to live an obscure life as a church musician. Only once in his sixty-five years did he actually take a job where his brilliance might bring him to the world's notice. For a while, he worked as Kapellmeister of the court of Prince Leopold. But such surroundings were a distraction to him. He soon left to accept a position as cantor at a church in Leipzig, where he would again be cloistered in his humble but beloved world of church music.

Masaaki Suzuki, founder of a school for Bach's music in Japan, says that, "Bach is teaching us the Christian concept of hope."[5] Yoshikazu Tokuzen, of Japan's National Christian Council, calls Bach nothing less than "a vehicle of the Holy Spirit." The revival his music is causing indeed confirms that. Suzuki says that "after each concert [of Bach's music], people crowd the podium wishing to talk to me about topics that are normally taboo in this society: death, for example. Then they inevitably ask me what 'hope' means to Christians . . . I believe that Bach has already converted tens of thousands of Japanese to the Christian faith."[6]

Bach's legacy is a sterling illustration of C. S. Lewis's maxim that the world does not need more Christian writers—it needs more good writers and composers, who are Christians. And when we produce art that is really good, art that reflects a biblical worldview, its richness will endure through the ages. Bach's work, life, and testimony of humility is a timeless example of the power of faith and music working together.

The Spiritual and Songs that Look to Heaven

For there they that carried us away captive required of us a song; and they that wasted us required of us mirth, saying, 'Sing us one of the songs of Zion.' How shall we sing the Lord's song in a strange land?

—PSALM 137:3–4

5. Sieman-Netto, "Why Nippon is Nuts," para. 8.

6. Ibid., para. 11.

We have also learned much about heaven, faith, singing, and worship from the traditional African-American spirituals that developed in our country in the eighteenth and nineteenth centuries. The simplicity, the message of hope, and their use of general language in expressing that hope have inspired many towards a deeper understanding of a relationship with Jesus Christ, and the hope of heaven that this relationship brings. The texts of the songs are a reminder of the eternal home for God's children. The particular conditions in which these songs were derived, during a reprehensive time in our country's history, communicate great hope in a place with conditions extremely different from this earthly home.

"Swing low, sweet chariot, comin' for to carry me home."

"Deep river, my home is over Jordan."

"I got a robe up in that kingdom, ain't that good news."

"There's no rain to wet you, O yes I want to go home."

"I know my robe's going to fit me well, I'm gonna lay down my heavy load, in the sweet by and by."

"Gonna lay down my burden, down by the riverside."

"I've got a robe, you've got a robe; when I get to heaven, gonna put on my robe and shout all over God's heaven."

"The gosel train's a comin', get on board little children."

"My Lord calls me . . . the trumpet sounds with in my soul. I ain't got long to stay here. Steel away to Jesus, steel away, home."

"This world's not my home, this world's a howling wilderness, this world's not my home."

André Thomas speaks about performing spirituals and gives the context for two spirituals: "Oh, What a Beautiful City" and "In Bright Mansions Above."

> The common thematic element between these two spirituals is a description of heaven. For the slave, these songs would likely have come as a reaction to the description of heaven in the Book of Revelation, with its streets of gold and golden slippers. While they still include a prominent theme of being comforted by the prospect of another home, here the focus is on how different this place is from their lives. Yes, the plantations had a certain beauty, but even the

road leading to the big house was just a dusty, dirt road. Here we have streets of gold.[7]

Secular Worldview of Christian Music

How can we expect a society that loves so many types of diverse music to separate the instilled, and usually original, intentions from their minds if we continue to replicate those secular styles in our corporate worship?

For even a novice music lover, and especially a trained one, the musical style, the song, and the secular icon of the sound being replicated is easily recognizable. Unfortunately, a majority of contemporary Christian musical styles are often not original musical forms—they have mostly been replicated from pop culture. The contrast of Christian music, as the world now sees it is through the pop culture and media, is the unique and historical approach to church music—what should be classified as *sacred music*. Historic church music has often had a sensibility of being geared to a sacred expression of faith, rather than an individual Christian expression. However, in the modern worldview the new contemporary paradigm is the norm for Christian music that often is communicated as an individual expression of worship. As a result of this, it appears that the secular attitude towards modern Christian music is perhaps even more negatively viewed than the traditional forms had previously been. Even in the late 1950s these trends were in play, according to Tozer,

> In our day we must be dramatic about everything. We don't want God to work unless he can make a theatrical production of it. We want him to come dressed in costumes with a beard and with a staff. We want him to play a part according to our ideas. Some of us even demand that he provide a colorful setting and fireworks as well![8]

Though many claim that traditional forms of worship and music lack warmth, vision, sustainability or understandability, the new issues often question the authenticity—from those who write the music to those leading it, cliché forms, overt sensationalism, its entertainment-driven approach, and an overall skewed view of an authentic Christian life. Musicians who have been part of church music often are working in other musical spheres

7. Thomas, *Way Over in Beulah Lan'*, 136.

8. Tozer, *Tozer on Worship*, 99.

outside the church and are exposed to many people and behaviors contrary to Scriptures. Churches have noticed this and have helped to equip musicians and to be mindful of how the leadership of music in worship must be consistent with the teachings of the church. Bob Kauflin has been very influential in training church musicians as worship leaders in the church and has helped the church musician develop a Christian authenticity that is consistent with the church and one's lifestyle outside the church.

> Whatever standards others might use to judge our ministry, God is concerned that we be faithful. Faithfulness means firmly adhering to the observance of a duty, keeping your word, fulfilling your obligations. It involves being loyal, constant, and reliable. Being faithful means fulfilling the desires of another. *We* don't define our ministry; *God* does.[9]

The leadership of church music has a profound testimony on how others view the church, her ministry, and her authenticity. Being a great musician, or being up to date with cultural trends are not the core matters of being an influence in a dark and broken world. Church musicians who are not in line with the doctrine of the gospel communicate poorly on the priorities of worship. Tozer makes a poignant challenge:

> In this day when shimmering personalities carry on the Lord's work after the methods of the entertainment world, it is refreshing to associate for a moment even in the pages of a book with a sincere and humble man who keeps his own personality out of sight and place the emphasis upon the inworking of God. It is our belief that the evangelical movement will continue to drift farther and farther from the New Testament position unless its leadership passes from the modern religious star to the self-effacing saint who asks for no praise and seeks no place, happy only when the glory is attributed to God and himself forgotten.[10]

Furthermore, depictions of popular Christian music by the secular media reveals the sarcastic attitude that is perceived by some in the non-Christian world. *South Park*, for example, is a crude and satirical comedy cartoon that is known for its brash perceptions of everyday real life. One particular episode, with all its foul language and secular slang, portrayed how the Christian music industry has a built-in audience of all Christians, and all it takes to make it big is to produce schmaltzy, lame music with

9. Kauflin, *Worship Matters*, 58.

10. Tozer, *Tozer on Worship*, 124.

lyrics that have simple, sentimental Christian jargon. The kids in this epi-sode take secular love songs and substitute "I love you, baby" with "I love you, Jesus," and they make it to the top Christian song on the charts. This seems to be a pretty sad portrayal of the world's view towards sacred music.

Music says much about our understanding of God, and also says much about what a given church may believe about God. Even the pagans know our modus operandi. This is not good for the church universal. The church ultimately has the control of dictating through its regular practice of worship how the world perceives our practices. With music being such a huge factor in the secular viewpoint of the church, it will obviously have a factor in the speculation of what heaven will be like because of the associa-tion with how we carry out the promise of hope through worship on earth.

CHAPTER 10

Musical Content

Great religious music texts deal with the great mysteries of life; the music to which they are set, exactly because of its non-specific nature, is uniquely qualified to illumine these ponderings on the meaning of life, on love, and loss, on suffering and transcendence. This is empowerment indeed: great truths of physical energy plus imaginative vision plus human consolation are experienced through great music.

—ALICE PARKER[1]

A GROWING DISPARITY IN church music issues is of church leaders misunderstanding each other. Often, it seems that the highly educated, classically trained musicians that are called to church music are valued for their contribution to the coordination of musical activities, but sometimes are not a part of the whole music process in the church. My experience has been one in which my philosophy of music ministry is mistaken for a personal preference on all matters musical. Musicians who value the role of rich hymnody, choirs, and organs are classified as "musical snobs" who will not budge in matters of trying to expand our musical acceptance of other forms of music, especially ones used in worship.

On the other hand, the calling and ordination of musicians to the church embraces the value of the training, understanding, and contribution of that musician's experience. While we should not expect all congregants to reach the same level of musical understanding as our trained and called

1. Parker, *Melodious Accord*, 23.

church musicians, we should allow the expectations of their experience to set the bar for higher musical enlightenment in the church. This, in turn, parallels with our expectation of spiritual development, biblical growth and knowledge, and how we set overall expectations of our faith, doing and being something greater in our own lives and in the world around us. If we continually allow the standard for church, its music, and everything else, to be dictated by cultural standards and not strive toward a greater understanding of the art that is set forth by those in that area, we unfortunately can miscommunicate the gospel message.

Likewise, pastors and those who are often disgruntled with the music of the church may have missed some points. While there are church musicians who are slaves to their preferred form, there are music leaders in churches who strive for excellence in presentation, content, and spiritual awareness. The call for the church musician is to be well grounded in understanding, to pray constantly for unity and for clarity in selecting music, and to be open to looking at and evaluating new forms of music. We should do so to understand where people in our churches are coming from, so that we have an opportunity to discuss the characteristics of music and teach the mechanics and details of why a certain song may not be fit for a corporate gathering of worship. This takes lots of time, research, and patience.

It is often difficult for professional musicians to understand the desires of the laity and pastors. It is equally or more challenging for them to understand the musicians. I deduce that this breakdown often happens over misunderstanding—the inflexibility of both parties to understand. Church musicians have developed over the past few decades a defense of what they believe is right. These are essentially the traditionalists and those who desire music beyond choirs and organs. Basically, we cannot say that one is right or one is wrong. However, as I have pointed out, there are valid points to the use of choirs and various instruments that will mimic heavenly worship. Likewise, bad choirs and organists are perhaps a worse testimony of the church's mission than any new forms of music in church can be. Quality of musical presentation aside, the real value of music in worship is based on the quality of the music and the texts.

Deep Worship

One church, Redeemer Presbyterian Church in New York City, is used as an example of how the church can focus on rich content in the book *Deep*

Church. "Deep" is certainly an important goal in the content of our worship. Belcher tells us how this is accomplished:

> It all starts with how we frame it [worship] . . . we attempt to hold the Bible, the tradition and our cultural context in tension, allowing them to inform every part of our worship service. Since the Bible does not give us enough information to construct a worship service, we must fill in the blanks. We are told in the Bible to sing songs, but we are not given tunes, or told what kind of lyrics the songs should have or how emotionally intense the experience should be . . . In order to be faithful we must draw on not only Scripture but tradition as well. But we also draw on our cultural sensitivities and our desire to "worship before the nations," making sure that our worship is accessible to an outsider. Keeping all three—Bible, tradition, and culture—in mind, we are able to craft a worship service that is neither irrelevant nor syncretistic.[2]

Pastors and musicians, both, can come to deeper understanding about the value of music in worship by simply evaluating, honestly, the valid points listed, and by understanding why something different may be particularly useful in a given context. Following are some of the things the church musician must consider when planning worship.

Relevance: Old or New

Church musicians must first recognize that there are wonderful new hymns and songs being written. There are great texts and tunes for any congregation with any musical accompaniments to use or even adapt to a service. Many of the modern hymns being written can be used with a band or organ, or piano or guitar. Some of the good ones work best with tender accompaniment (guitar or piano) over grand accompaniment (brass or organ). Likewise, pastors must remember that many of the texts and tunes and songs written over the last 1,000 years have endured. The testimony of the church through creative texts and music still has a vast influence in our modern context. The output over these many years is vast. When one thinks of the balance of the historical contribution of the past to the proportion of songs in the last ten years, the understanding of the importance of what is perceived as old, is now considered a part of the narrative of Christianity. Now, not all texts written more than one hundred years

2. Belcher, *Deep Church*, 137.

ago make sense with our modern use of language. However, that should not stop the church from looking at those and considering their impact. Are there words that can be substituted? For instance, many churches often teach about the significance of the word "Ebenezer" in the hymn "Come, Thou Fount of Ev'ry Blessing."

Likewise, and even more daunting, is understanding and balancing old music with new music. Musicians need to be realistic about determining when an old tune does not carry weight in comparison with the wealth of tunes and songs that are well-crafted and express musical thought with integrity and expression. Oftentimes this decision comes when selecting tunes for old words. With the popular movement of using old texts with new tunes, there may be more than one tune associated with a given text. This is where musicians should look at the structure of the music and ask the questions raised in criteria for a good hymn or song. For instance, "Abide With Me" has a tune ("Eventide") that is well known and has the characteristics of a good hymn, which were previously listed. In having to choose the older tune over the newer one, I would say let's stick with the one that works. However, if a text like "A Debtor To Mercy Alone" is being questioned, I can honestly say that the older tune in our hymnal lacks expression and shape and does not express the sentiment of the text, so let's find a better tune. Asking the question of which is better—old or new—can certainly help determine desirable content for worship. We serve our congregations well when we seek to make choices that are grounded in important older texts and tunes, and eagerly seek new creativity being produced currently.

Quality: Good or Bad

Both proponents of new and old must also remember that in every generation and era there are good words and not so good words, bad tunes and not so bad tunes. We have already addressed characteristics of a good tune for congregational singing. Other considerations must be made in selecting all music for the service, including solos, instrumental or choir selections, for example. Musicians should speak towards the quality of the music and have influence on choices that represent the collective narrative of music.

It is not surprising that many new texts lack depth in teaching or even basic expression of human emotion. Pastors should understand the theological accuracy and soundness of what the congregation is singing and have influence with the musicians in determining which texts are theologically astute and which are not. Many times when something does not work in the repertoire, there is something better available.

This question of "good or bad" is the most subjective raised here, and therefore can be difficult to determine. Just as we will rely on the expertise of pastors to guide and monitor the use of texts and prayers in the service we should seek the experience of the collective contributions of church musicians. Though a dramatic shift has developed among church musicians, and mainstream acceptance and perception of music has been altered in the past fifty years, the historical pattern of emphasizing content is evident through the vast hymns and texts that have been sustained in worship for many hundreds of years.

Context: Individual or Corporate

This one should be rather easy to determine. Sometimes, though, what is meant to be corporate praise is misunderstood by some who may not fully comprehend why we sing in church, nor the great joy of participating in robust congregational song. This is an area where Christian entertainment has blurred the expectation of the church in what music is suitable for worship. Unfortunately, many of the songs produced or written by Christian artists, no matter how good the text or music may be, may not be fully grasped by the congregation as a whole nor should be sung by large groups. The real importance of congregational singing is that it represents the whole body of Christ praising God and responding to his goodness. The purpose of music is not to be in lieu of the representative voice of "the church." Therefore, it is important that everyone sing and the difficulty or range of the music, complexity of rhythms or other musical nuance often in the contemporary worship music or even some classical melodies can make it difficult for the congregation to participate.

Sentiment: Heaven or Earth

Finally, we evaluate the sentiment of music and what it communicates about our great and awesome God. When the church begins to think about the simple statement of C. S. Lewis—aim at heaven and you get earth thrown in; aim at earth and you get neither—it seems indisputable that simple choices in the music of the church can contain aspirations beyond human understanding. Even more so is the opportunity to bring heaven to earth through our music. The levels of creativity that have been carried out by God's feeble creatures will pale when compared to the heavenly music we will one day experience. But as we have seen to this point in developing a music philosophy with an eye towards heaven, there are many ways of experiencing and worshipping God and many forms of music that aid us.

Up until a year or so ago, I believed that understanding music outside one's experience in church was based upon spiritual depth or desire for just that: an experience. However, I experienced something in my office that I will never forgot one March afternoon. I was meeting with a young man who was interested in assisting with our contemporary service. This young man was a fine professional guitarist who had served in a commercial Christian music industry and whose entire experience in church music had been in the paradigm of new worship songs led by band in a casual setting. I was astonished at how few great hymns this man knew, so I could tell that our setting of worship was something quite different. One of my choirs was preparing parts two and three of George F. Handel's masterful and classic oratorio *Messiah*. I was sitting at my desk and happened to have the recordings on my music player and began to play "Worthy Is the Lamb," the final movement of this timeless work. I asked him if he had ever heard it and he said he had not. The next few minutes of sitting and listening, without any speaking, was transformational. This man was weeping to the music he was hearing. As the piece finished and he looked up, I will never forget his expression. In his very cool and hipster sort of way he said, "Whoa, that was epic."

It was at that moment that I understood the transformational power of music, particularly its ability to "take us to the heavenlies." From that moment, I began to think about where music can take us. I began to think about its power and how mysteriously God works through music and art, and its ability to communicate sentiments not easily expressed. It became clear that if I had a choice to play "Worthy Is the Lamb" from Handel's *Messiah* or a popular, modern setting of the same text for a person who did not know the gospel truth, that it would be the classic setting from *Messiah*. It was then in my journey that I realized that the choices of music I make can be transformational. It was then that I began to carry out a music ministry that uses music to focus on heaven.

We live in a day and age where there are countless options of music and texts and, many times, one can be overwhelmed with the vast repertoire available for use in the church. Though I still believe that people will respond to all types of music in some way or another, I am fully aware of the ways music can transport us.

PART 3

Church Music that Aspires: Heaven at Work

What does Christ give to his church in worship?

Unto this catholic visible church, Christ has given the ministry, oracles, and ordinances of God, for the gathering and perfecting of this saints, in this life, to the end of the world: and does by his own presence and Spirit, according to his promise, make them effectual.

—WESTMINSTER CONFESSIONAL OF FAITH, 25:3

GOD HAS GIVEN US all we need to worship. He has given us music, the gifts and abilities to worship him. The challenge for us as his children is the *perfection* and *perfecting* of what he has given us and called us to. Charles Haddon Spurgeon speaks of the matter of practicing for heaven.

> It is said of all these worshippers that they learned the song before they went there. At the end of the third verse it is said, "No man could learn that song but the hundred and forty and four thousand, which were redeemed from the earth." Brethren, we must begin heaven's song here below, or else we shall never sing it above. The choristers of heaven have all had rehearsals upon earth, before they sing in that orchestra. You think that, die when you may, you will go to heaven, without being prepared. Nay, sir; heaven is a prepared place for a prepared people, and unless you are "made

meet to be partakers of the inheritance of the saints in light," you can never stand there among them.[1]

The current issues in church music and worship are ones that can draw us closer to heaven and ones that perhaps keep us on earth, as well. The standards from Scripture and our historical models that point to heaven offer inspiration for how we can better carry out the music of the church on earth.

What are the issues we face on earth that keep us from attaining a higher and more heavenly view of worship? What in our worship is missing and what causes that?

> It certainly is true that hardly anything is missing from our churches these days—except the most important thing. We are missing the genuine and sacred offering of ourselves and our worship to the God and Father of our Lord Jesus Christ. We have been surging forward. We are building great churches and large congregations. We are boasting about high standards and we are talking a lot about revival. But I have a question and it is not just rhetoric: What has happened to our worship? I wish that we might get back to worship again. Then when people come into the church they will instantly sense that they have come among holy people, God's people. They can testify, "a true God is in this place."[2]

This section will look at the issues of pragmatism that often keep our worship aspirations grounded in earthly standards and then how we can aspire towards heavenly worship and the heavenly standard of what determines beauty. We will explore the means we communicate the Gospel truth through music, as well as the simple fact that we are creating music in the "image of God." The intent here is to raise questions, explore trends and patterns, and to help church musicians, pastors, and leaders in the church to formulate their role in carrying out a heavenly vision of music and worship within the context God has called.

---

1. Spurgeon, "Heavenly Worship," part II, para. 6.
2. Tozer, *Whatever Happened to Worship*, 4–5.

CHAPTER 11

Communicating the Gospel through Music

Music is a fair and glorious gift from God. I am strongly persuaded that after theology there is no art that can be placed on a level with music; for besides theology, music is the only art capable of affording peace and joy of the heart.

—MARTIN LUTHER[1]

Music has the power to move a person between different realities: from a broken body into a soaring spirit, from a broken heart into the connection of shared love, from death into the memory and movement of life. Music has the power to touch the heart of a child with God.

—DEFORIA LANE[2]

Reverence and Awe

Many of the scriptural and historical sources we have examined instruct us to worship with "reverence and awe." These three words are used most often in defense of the former paradigms of music in the church. Traditionalists often claim that the newer paradigms lack reverence, among other things. Likewise, those leading the newer models have claimed that worship should

1. Lull and Russell, *Martin Luther's*, 188.

2. Lane, *Music as Medicine*, 92.

be a "celebration" and have felt the need to compensate by leading worship in a way that excites the congregation in a way the former models, those perceived as "stayed or too reverent," could not. Hart and Muether speak to the contrasting use of the word *celebration*:

> This word has a venerable history in worship, as when churches "celebrate" the Lord's Supper. But what happens when the meaning is altered, when celebrations suggests the high-fiving, champagne-spraying swagger of World Series champions or the exuberant and raucous festivities on New Year's Eve at Times Square? Of course there are other kinds of celebration, such as the dignity and gravity of a king's coronation or the simple solemnity of a church wedding. We must be mindful of these differences and not sanction by our language certain forms of celebration that are inappropriate for the church gathered for worship.[3]

So, why is reverence important? First of all, the definition of the word reverence alone reminds us that this is *an attitude of deep respect tinged with awe, and the outward manifestation of this feeling.* A part of the misunderstanding about reverence is that it is an "attitude" and the verb is the "outward manifestation" of this "attitude." The implication that reverence has in worship, and especially in music-making, is the attitude of how and to whom we regard the reverence. We may have respect and reverence for a king or a dignitary, while we may also have the same for someone to whom we are very close. Most likely, our attitude towards the dignitary will be very different from the person to whom we are closer. While reverence, as we know it, has mostly been manifested through strict obedience with posture, silence, even ritual gestures and such, the modern worship culture has expanded the attitude beyond the historic norms.

The difference seems to be in the view of the person to whom we are worshipping. While, there are many genuine affections offered to our God in a variety of forms, it is true that we worship a King. It is stated throughout Scripture that he reigns on high, and we have seen the pomp in which this regard has been held for generations. Fortunately, He is also our Friend, our Comforter, and our Redeemer. So, how do we show reverence and awe to such a King, with whom we are honored to have a personal relationship?

Perhaps the next word in this three-word phrase will tell us: *awe*. Again, the definition alone tells us that awe is *an overwhelming feeling of reverence, admiration, fear; produced by that which is grand, sublime,*

3. Hart and Muether, *With Reverence and Awe*, 23.

extremely powerful; and wonder that is inspired by authority or by the sacred or sublime.

Because of the power of music, there is a great challenge for those leading music in the church to seriously consider the need for reverence and awe. Music has the power to communicate the outward manifestation of reference and awe by the posture, admiration, and fear the music communicates. To look to heaven and to communicate reverence and awe through our music has great potential to guide the character and overall direction of what is presented to God by his children for public worship. The ways in which we evaluate our current trends and paradigms will impact the considerations we have made and should inspire us towards heavenly worship and music-making.

How Does Music Present the Gospel?

Should music in the corporate worship service be counter to culture or in the culture? The Word of God does not change, so why do we feel music must instantly change shape with each subsequent generation? The necessary subtle changes are passed on to each generation and historically have been based on greater understanding of God and the world, improvements, if you will. The recent shift in change for the church has reversed the cycle to simplify the methods of worship, teaching and discipleship for the sake of being relevant in the world. Church music trends strive to imitate the world rather than the informed premise of worship in heaven. Hart and Muether speak on the issues of the church and the world:

> The biblical distinction drawn between holiness and worldliness means that the church is by nature antithetical to the world. The church is at war with the world, and it has the duty to fight worldliness, a duty that we find throughout redemptive history. With the first promise of a redeemer in Genesis, God announced that all of history, from that point forward, would witness a cosmic battle between two camps. God declared . . . "I will put enmity between you (the serpent) and the woman, and between your seed and her seed; he shall bruise you on the head, and you shall bruise him on the heel."[4] The seed of the woman is the church, which is pitted against the seed of the serpent, that is, the world. The battle in view here is of an absolute spiritual antithesis between those chosen for

4. Gen 3:15.

life and those dead in sin, between the children of light and the children of darkness.[5]

Likewise, the Bible warns the Christian of the importance of being different from the world. The implications for corporate worship music are:

> Do not love the world or the things in the world. If anyone loves the world, the love of the Father is not in him. For all that is in the world—the desires of the flesh and the desires of the eyes and pride in possessions—is not from the Father but is from the world. And the world is passing away along with its desires, but whoever does the will of God abides forever.[6]
>
> Now we have received not the spirit of the world, but the Spirit who is from God, that we might understand the things freely given us by God.[7]
>
> You adulterous people! Do you not know that friendship with the world is enmity with God? Therefore whoever wishes to be a friend of the world makes himself an enemy of God.[8]

Again, Hart and Muether speak to how the theological implications connect to corporate worship for the church:

> What does this have to do with worship? Perhaps the connection is not immediately obvious. One implication is that if the church is at war with the world, the wisdom and ways of the gospel will appear foolish to those who are enemies of God. As Paul writes, "For the word of the cross is foolishness to those who are perishing, but to us who are being saved it is the power of God."[9] Another implication is that the contrast between the church and world will be most obvious when the church is at worship. The church in worship should be like that described by Paul in 1 Thessalonians, that is, turning "from idols to serve a living and true God."[10] The very act of worship, of assembling in the presence of God, therefore, is simultaneously the church's renunciation of the world. Worship is a subversive and counter-cultural act of an alien

---

5. Hart and Muether, *With Reverence and Awe*, 210.

6. 1 John 2:15–17.

7. 1 Cor 2:12.

8. Jas 4:4.

9. 1 Cor 1:18.

10. 1 Thess 1:9.

people who, forsaking the world, listen to the voice of her master saying, "follow me."[11]

One cultural evidence at work in the church is the attitude towards *old things*. Modern culture emphasizes youth culture, new clothes, and new trends, especially new music. Though the Bible encourages us to sing a new song, there is even stronger emphasis on singing psalms—which most churches are far from—so why are we so intrigued by new songs, when we should be singing more psalms? Contrary to scrapping everything old, the Bible teaches a contradictory emphasis . . . to build on each generation.[12] Contemporary Christian music as we know it evidences a deliberate *newness* that is very contrasting to our historical consensus of solid church music. How can we do both without devaluing the principles of the other. Hart and Muether best summarize the implications for the church's worship and her music:

> . . . the church must be unapologetic in her worship. She must not cater to those bound to ridicule her ways as foolish. Christian worship is, in fact, a bold political act. It subverts the world's values by assigning glory and praise to the one whom the world despises. And as weak as the church at worship might appear to the watching world, the truth is that the powers of this world are no match for the power of God who is present among his people when they gather to sing praise, pray, and hear his Word. Moreover the church must reject the claim that worship is old-fashioned, irrelevant, and isolated from the "real world." For believers, the church at worship is the real world. The gathering of the saints in the holy of holies is the eschatological foretaste of the new heavens and the new earth, the reality to which all of history is headed. Of course, visitors to our churches should receive help in finding Joel in the Bible or knowing when to sit or stand. No one objects to this kind of sensitivity. But the world is predisposed to misunderstand the church. Christians cannot expect unbelievers to be comfortable in services of worship that are alien to the ways of the world. "User-friendly" or "seeker-sensitive" worship is not an option for the people of God. In fact, worship that demonstrates the separateness of the church is what Machen called "merciful unkindness" because it testifies to the world of the hope that is within us. If the

11. Hart and Muether, *With Reverence and Awe*, 12.

12. Ps 90.

world mocks us, so be it. True worship is for the church, not for the world.[13]

Corporate and Private Worship

The issues brought forth thus far are strictly in regard to music issues pertaining to corporate worship. Jeffrey Meyers says "If we want worship to be corporate (from the Latin *corpus*, "body"), then it must involve the entire local body of Christ, we must say and do things together."[14] That is to sing, pray, and read together. Monte Wilson describes the importance of liturgy in understanding corporate worship:

> The value of a thoughtfully considered liturgy is that it enforces the idea that we are worshipping as the church, not as individuals or home groups. We are the Ship of Orthodoxy, not three-hundred separate rafts in a lagoon. In many evangelical circles this is a great temptation. An individual may soar into the heavenlies and, oblivious to everything and everyone around him, dance and shout to his heart's content. However, when we gather as the church, we can never be oblivious to those around us.[15] A home group may sing, testify, confess, sing some more, laugh, break for coffee, and come back together for teaching; but when we gather as the church, we must remember we are in God's Throne Room, not our living room. This is not coffee with our buddies but a royal audience with the King of the universe. This is of particular relevance because so many Christians today approach church worship as an extension of their prayer closets.[16]

A significant part of the corporate gathering of worship is the music. The biblical approach to church music must consider its music as either suitable for corporate worship or as a vehicle for other intentions. Much of the music being produced for the purpose of Christian entertainment has value as an alternative to secular music that is filled with trashy content. Most of this is written for commercial intent and by nature does not necessarily fit a mold for corporate worship. It is often soloistic in nature and is not written with the intent to be sung as a corporate offering of worship.

13. Hart and Muether, *With Reverence and Awe*, 96.

14. Meyers, *The Lord's Service*, 131.

15. 1 Cor 14.

16. Wilson, "Church-O-Rama," 76.

The use of commercialized Christian music should seriously be considered before being used to aid corporate worship. There are many implications to consider for appropriate corporate worship music as opposed to what we may select for our own entertainment, private worship, youth or college gathering, or just personal preference.

If we select music for *corporate* worship based on one generation's personal music preference, we have missed the beauty of serving a multigenerational congregation. While some new music has strength in the context of college campuses in the way it is exciting the hearts of our young people towards solid texts, consideration must be given to its generational appeal. We in essence say—one generation is more important than the other—instead of saying we believe the music of the church should be unique to the church (its own musical language, if you will) and not trying to meet the constantly changing secularly influenced personal tastes of a single generation. We will continue to fail as a church because we will always be behind the curve. Look at start up churches from twenty years ago that based their philosophy on pragmatically trying to reach "the unchurched" or "overchurched." They now have to reinvent themselves in order to reach the next generation and their speculated "preference" of what a church should be to their target group.

The problem with this generational approach is that we do miss teaching these students the tunes that are more fully embraced by the church universal. It is, therefore, the duty of the church to train up young people with the tools they need for worship that is a consensual belief of what is good for corporate worship. If each generation continues to produce its own music without also learning some form of intergenerational church music, we will continue the trend of changing the churches music based on generational preference. The church must be committed to something that will at least last through a complete generation.

Our new church leaders who claim that historic, liturgical church worship is outdated, I am convinced, have been influenced by the quick visible successes of the pop culture church. I fear we have failed to look at all these implications that the modern churches fail to see, and we are now seeing pieces of the contemporary church culture sneak into churches that have allowed themselves to be influenced by the worldly, mainline church. These churches have now established their own "culture" that is spreading across churches. The trends are: bands, songs, hip clothing, meetings in gyms (purposely not because of lack of resources), hand raising, dancing, swaying, closing eyes, and all the like. I would argue that the contemporary church is blurring the lines of private and corporate worship. These characteristics are all *personal* expressions of worship, not *corporate.*

The Bible makes clear the importance of gathering for corporate worship—and the unique ways that the church worships together.[17] The Bible also points out private worship, particularly in psalms. If we look at the psalms of David, there are categories of psalms: psalms of corporate lament, praise and thanksgiving; and likewise psalms of individual lament, praise, and thanksgiving. In fact, David is a great example of an expressive worshipper—he was musical, he wrote psalms for both settings, and he is known as the one who danced before the Lord. I would ask in what context did he dance? It was in the streets, not in the temple, and it even embarrassed his wife.

This is something to look at—should our expressions of public worship be individualized? As Christians, we should be aware of our environment. We should always worship with reverence in our heart, but what should our bodies be displaying, especially in public? Do we alienate people, especially seekers, by allowing our private expressions to draw attention to ourselves?

If the music leads us into questionable areas of how we should approach God, should we be encouraging that? I am convinced that the sounds, emotions, and music of the contemporary church encourage private worship traits in the corporate setting when certain forms of devotional music are used. This trend seems to be driven by musical selection, musical presentation, and overall environment.

I also fear that because the trend stems from charismatic traditions that have now made this behavior their cultural norm, that it lacks some sincerity because it is expected and encouraged by the leadership and by general peer influence. I would not question the authenticity and/or sincerity of some of those who are expressing themselves, but I have become suspicious of the overall culture. When told to raise your hands or close your eyes by the worship leaders, I cannot believe that the expression can be a sincere corporate act of worship.

Private worship, home worship, and those gathered for college fellowship are all legitimate opportunities for personal expression of worship. However, the corporate worship setting calls for greater demands and details from the church. The church should take seriously the implications of what we present in corporate worship. The opportunity of congregational

17. Isa 6; Rev 4.

singing in corporate worship to display the glory and grandeur of heaven is expressed in Revelation 14:1–3:

> And I looked, and, lo, a Lamb stood on the Mount Zion, and with him an hundred forty and four thousand, having his Father's name written in their foreheads. And I heard a voice from heaven, as the voice of many waters, and as the voice of a great thunder: and I heard the voice of harpers harping with their harps; And they sung as it were a new song before the throne, and before the four beasts, and the elders; and no man could learn that song but the hundred and forty and four thousand, which were redeemed from the earth.

The beautiful experience of singing corporately in worship can only be eclipsed by what we expect the singing in heaven to be. Spurgeon expounds on this text most eloquently and offers the most profound case for corporate singing and how it prepares us for heaven:

> ". . . singing *how loud*! It is said to be "like the voice of many waters." Have you never heard the sea roar, and the fulness thereof? Have you never walked by the sea-side, when the waves were singing, and when every little pebble-stone did turn chorister, to make up music to the Lord God of hosts? And have you never in time of storm beheld the sea, with its hundred hands, clapping them in gladsome adoration of the Most High? Have you never heard the sea roar out his praise, when the winds were holding carnival—perhaps singing the dirge of mariners, wrecked far out on the stormy deep, but far more likely exalting God with their hoarse voice, and praising him who makes a thousand fleets sweep over them in safety, and writes his furrows on their own youthful brow? Have you never heard the rumbling and booming of ocean on the shore, when it has been lashed into fury and has been driven upon the cliffs? If you have, you have a faint idea of the melody of heaven. It was "as the voice of many waters." But do not suppose that it is the whole of the idea. It is not the voice of one ocean, but the voice of many, that is needed to give you an idea of the melodies of heaven. You are to suppose ocean piled upon ocean, sea upon sea—the Pacific piled upon the Atlantic, the Arctic upon that, the Antarctic higher still, and so ocean upon ocean, all lashed to fury, and all sounding with a mighty voice the praise of God. Such is the singing of heaven.
>
> Or if the illustration, fails to strike, take another. We have mentioned here two or three times the mighty falls of Niagara. They can be heard at a tremendous distance, so awful is their

sound. Now, suppose waterfalls dashing upon waterfalls, cataracts upon cataracts, Niagaras upon Niagaras, each of them sounding forth their mighty voices, and you have got some idea of the singing of paradise. "I heard a voice like the voice of many waters." Can you not hear it? Ah! if our ears were opened we might almost cast the song. I have thought sometimes that the voice of the Aeolian harp, when it has swollen out grandly, was almost like an echo of the songs of those who sing before the throne; and on the summer eve, when the wind has come in gentle zephyrs through the forest, you might almost think it was the floating of some stray notes that had lost their way among the harps of heaven, and come down to us, to give us some faint foretaste of that song which hymns out in mighty peals before the throne of the Most High. But why so loud? The answer is, because there are so many there to sing. Nothing is more grand than the singing of multitudes. Many have been the persons who have told me that they could but weep when they heard you sing in this assembly, so mighty seemed the sound when all the people sang—

"Praise God from whom all blessings flow."

And, indeed, there is something very grand in the singing of multitudes. I remember hearing 12,000 sing on one occasion in the open air. Some of our friends were then present, when we concluded our service with that glorious hallelujah. Have you ever forgotten it? It was indeed a mighty sound; it seemed to make heaven itself ring again. Think, then, what must be the voice of those who stand on the boundless plains of heaven, and with all their might shout, "Glory and honour and power and dominion unto him that sitteth on the throne, and to the Lamb for ever and ever."

On reason, however, why the song is so loud is a very simple one, namely, because all those who are there think themselves bound to sing the loudest of all. You know our favorite hymn—

"Then loudest of the crowd I'll sing,
While heav'n's resounding mansions ring
With shouts of sov'reign grace."[18]

Within a Biblical Framework

There are many biblical principles that support a higher approach to church music:

18. Spurgeon, "Heavenly Worship," part III.

Heavenly view of worship.

In every instance that the Bible addresses worship and specifically music, it is with the aim of heaven. Even though the church on earth lives simultaneously in two dimensions, the heavenly and the earthly, her worship is focused on the heavenly realm. From a physical standpoint, we gather for worship in a place of worship. But in a mystery, our worship is conducted in the heavenliest. Present are: God the Father, God the Son, God the Holy Spirit, the holy angels, and the saints enrolled in heaven. In corporate worship the church on earth joins the church in heaven (in fact, it's just one church!) in praise and thanksgiving to the Blessed Trinity. [19] There are numerous scriptural passages that describe worship in the heavens. Let me refer briefly to two of them, one in the Old Testament, one in the New.

In Isaiah 6:1–7, we see worship in heaven through the eyes of the Prophet Isaiah who lived in the years surrounding 700 BC. He was caught up into the heavenly dimension and describes for us what took place. He says, "I saw the Lord sitting on a throne, high and lifted up, and the train of His robe filled the temple." Present as well were the seraphim singing: "Holy, Holy, Holy is the Lord of hosts; The whole earth is full of His glory." Isaiah goes on to describe a heavenly altar, the smoke of incense, and the door of entrance. It is significant that one of the seraphim takes a set of tongs and removes a coal from the altar and with it touches Isaiah's lips, saying, "Behold this has touched your lips, your iniquity is taken away, and your sin is purged." Just as Isaiah experienced the liturgy of heaven, so we, too, joined to Christ and risen with him in the heavens, may enter his presence in heavenly worship.

The New Testament passage is the twelfth chapter of Hebrews. The passage begins by reminding us that "we are surrounded" by a great cloud of witnesses. These witnesses are the saints who have gone on before us to their rest, in this case, those the author of Hebrews has just mentioned in the previous chapter: the "greats" of Old Testament times. Then, toward the end of Hebrews 12, we read again of our ascent as Christians into the heavenly realm. For we have come "to the city of the living God, the heavenly Jerusalem, to an innumerable company of angels, to the general assembly and church of the firstborn who are registered in heaven, to God the Judge of all, to the spirits of just men made perfect, to Jesus the Mediator of the New Covenant." It would be difficult to mistake what is happening here, would it

19. Rev 4.

not? The church on earth is actually stepping into the heavenly dimension for worship. The Lord is present as are the saints and the angels—the entire host of the church in heaven. I cannot imagine why any church would shrink from any opportunity to experience this celestial encounter with the Triune God every time her doors are opened.

Corporate worship in heaven . . .

Involves choirs, instruments and angels. Scripture has demonstrated that the music will be on a mass scale. The singing will be rich (because all of our voices will be perfect . . . better than the best trained voice on earth) and the instruments will proclaim his glory.[20] Everything will be beautiful (because our minds will be cleared of personal preference) and all beauty will be for the sole glory of God. But, while on earth, we have to work with the limitations we have. Therefore, if we want to offer God our best, we have to make choices. Choices that either reconcile our view of our best worship to God or that serves another purpose.

Spiritual giftedness.

Christianity supports a philosophy of people creating music and art as a personal expression of faith, even those with just novice ability. God has designed us to create and all Christians should feel the liberty to "create art" for the glory of God. However, just as many in our congregations may have a passion and gift of preaching, we don't just let them have the pulpit because they have a gift. There is a place for them to use there gifts in settings *other than corporate worship*. Likewise with music, if we follow all biblical principles of giving God our best, this will include the actual musicians and the actual music we use in our *corporate* consensus as the best we have to offer.

Stewardship.

The principles of giving God our best in all aspects of life would seem to be most poignant in worship. Each congregation should offer the best of that given congregation's *corporate* experience. This would include the resources (if you have instruments, they should be used to the best of

20. 1 Chr 23; Ps 33, 98, 150; Matt 9:23, 11, 17; 1 Cor 13, 14.

the church's ability), personnel (if you have gifted musicians trained and called to lead the church's *corporate* worship, they should be used), and the best of the church's collective understanding of *the best* available. This is good stewardship.

. . . within the legitimate preferred cultural expressions of our people.

Because there is more evidence for a biblical approach to music that incorporates excellence and an approach that ascends to the heavens, I would argue that biblical worship is a far greater matter than cultural relevance. Of course, within reason, worship should be culturally relevant. We are not at the same place as the reformers were 500 years ago in trying to fight for the liturgy to be in the actual vernacular language. We are not talking about the difference of moving from all Latin to English. We are talking about presentation of worship. Should it be compromised based on personal expressions of one given group or should it reflect an entire culture? We are not just trying to justify our legitimate preferences, but we are trying to display the *entire* gospel truth through our corporate worship.

Beauty.

Thomas A. Troeger speaks of the *necessity of beauty* in his book *Music as Prayer*. He asks

> Why should churches budget money for musical instruments, directors, and organists in a time of financial stress? Because, as Christ said to the temptor when he asked to turn stones into bread, "One does not live by bread alone, but by every word that comes from the mouth of God."[21] Every word of God includes not only the petition,: Give us this day our daily bread," but also the prayer of the psalmist "to behold the beauty of the Lord, and to inquire in his temple."[22] Of course, we live by bread. Of course, the financial crunch matters to all of us. But we need beauty as much as we need bread. It would be cruel if just when people were desperate for some glimmer of meaning and hope, the church faltered by starving them of beauty. Beauty is balm to the wounded

21. Matt 4:4.

22. Ps 27:4.

and world-wearied souls that are coming to church during these troubled times. When we play or sing or direct beautiful music, we are offering a ministry of healing.[23]

Tozer challenges us in the importance of understanding beauty:

> I hope that we will remove from our hearts every ugly thing and every unbeautiful thing and every dead thing and every unholy thing that might prevent us from worshipping the Lord Jesus Christ in the beauty of holiness. Now I am quite sure that this kind of thing is not popular. The world does not want to hear it and the half-saved churches of the evangelical fold do not want to hear it. They want to be entertained while they are edified. Entertain me and edify me without pain.[24]

Transcendence and Immanence

The discussion in evangelical churches about the roles of transcendence and immanence in worship is one that often separates the two to justify the practice of traditional worship or contemporary worship. The issue is one that one cannot exist without the other. To separate them and then put them in terms of human relevance or experience, especially in attempts to market worship as two separate experiences, has missed the beauty found in each that cannot be achieved independently. It seems that transcendence leads to immanence; and immanence in this context is the work of God in an individual's heart, not his surroundings or entrapments. To mistake an intimate experience as immanence could pose some serious fundamental questions to our historic roots on these topics.

> Due to the work of the philosopher Immanuel Kant in the eighteenth century, many thinkers began to question whether we could ever know anything about the transcendent realm. This was based on an unbiblical view of transcendence, one that says God is so "wholly other" that it is impossible for His creation to communicate with Him at all. In any case, these ideas trickled down into theology, and through a variety of alterations they produced a new emphasis on immanence. However, the immanence promoted was also an unbiblical one, which basically said that God is so closely identified with His creation as to be virtually indistinguishable

23. Troeger, *Music as Prayer*, 62.

24. Tozer, *Tozer on Worship*, 104.

from it. The new focus on immanence is known as "immanentism" and ultimately amounts to pantheism.

The result for Christology was to remove any sense that Jesus was unique as an incarnation of God. If all is God, then God is all, not only Jesus. At best, the philosopher G. W. F. Hegel said, Jesus is a picture of what it means that humanness and deity are ultimately one. This humanization of God and deification of man is antithetical to biblical orthodoxy.

The immanentism we have discussed today is still with us. The New Age idea that we are all divine is a further alteration of immanentistic thought and also draws upon Eastern religions. We must be on guard against any view that would make God identical to His creation, for then He would be identified with the wickedness His creation has promulgated. To lose God's transcendence is to lose any hope that He will overcome the evil of this world.[25]

The wisdom of these theological principles, is perhaps, the needed safeguard for the church in interpreting how God works in worship. We obviously hold high regard for theological issues, and this subject could be the factor that dictates what the limit to emotional human experience of worship should be and likewise emphasizes the high regard for the intellectual impact that triggers our heart. To have a high intellectual understanding of God (transcendence) prompts an imminent experience that I suspect can only be found in one's heart. To separate the two and to deduce that separate worship environments prompt one over the other needs to be revisited.

To separate immanence and use it as an independent quality of worship poses other questions. Even the secular interpretation of immanence categorizes it as *being generally associated with mysticism and mystical sects but most religions have elements of both immanent and transcendent belief in their doctrines.* Likewise, their description of transcendence independently *is a trance-like condition or state of being that surpasses physical existence and in one form is also independent of it.*[26] Even secular interpretation balances the need for both. When looked at individually, these descriptions would associate Christianity with some pretty unorthodox faiths. But together they work as a condition of an individual experience of God.

Lastly, I would argue both transcendence and immanence cannot be simply coerced by external conditions or human experiences. These are both areas that are only experienced with the presence of the Holy Spirit in

25. Sproul, "Denying God's Transcendence."

26. As found in Merriam Webster's Collegiate Dictionary.

both one's mind and heart. No human or worldly sentiment can transcend the heart of an individual without the divine presence of God. And to be honest, I feel confident that no style of music will do this on its own merits. If we expect any music to accomplish either trait, we have sorely misunderstood God's ability to work in the human heart.

Worship Leadership

We have addressed the need and biblical foundation required for credibility and authenticity of church musicians. One particular trend in the modern evangelical church is the concept or position of "worship leader"—the one leading the music for the corporate body. First, this misnomer perhaps communicates, because the one "leading the worship" is a musician, that worship is therefore strictly music. I make this point in our new members class first thing as I, the music director, am to teach the portion on worship.

> When music is seen as a means to encounter God, worship leaders and musicians are vested with a priestly role. They become the ones who bring us into the presence of God rather than Jesus Christ who alone has already fulfilled that role. Understandably, when a worship leader or band doesn't help me experience God they have failed and must be replaced. On the other hand, when we believe that they have successfully moved us into God's presence they will attain in our minds a status that is far too high for their own good.[27]

Historically, the titles of pastor, or choir director, or music director have more specifically identified the roles the person is fulfilling. Ron Mann makes a poignant thesis on Hebrews 12:1–2 that particularly reminds us that Christ is the worship leader, "This passage . . . has tremendous and far-reaching implications for how we understand the Church, her Head and her worship . . . the Lord Jesus is living and active in our midst as the Mediator of God's truth and the Leader of our worship."[28] While we certainly know of no true leader of music or worship or preaching in any church that will dispute it is Christ who leads our worship, Mann reminds us of the humility required to lead worship and that any title we bear is not ours.

27. Pruitt, "Is Your Church Worship More Pagan Than Christian?" para 7.

28. Man, *Proclamation and Praise*, xi.

Boundless dignity is given to the roles of both preacher and worship leader, when it is considered that in both one is representing Jesus Christ, who is the true Agent and Mediator of those ministries. And this truth also calls for great humility as we exercise those ministries. It is not *my* ministry of teaching, *my* preaching ministry, *my* worship ministry—it is Christ's, and I am merely standing in for Him, so to speak, as His channel and mouthpiece, in the power of the Holy Spirit. . . . Calvin reminds us that "Christ heeds our praise, and is the chief Conductor of our hymns."[29] Even the common title of "worship leader" seems a misnomer when one realizes that it is Christ Himself who is the leader of His brethren's worship.[30]

Worship Atmosphere

I would add that just as the actual space where worship takes place has been a high calling for generations past—to give the best—as in the great cathedrals of Europe, music likewise, sets the tone and atmosphere for worship, perhaps more than any other factor. I strongly believe that music is emphasized as such an important part of worship because of its likeness to the presence of God. Music cannot be touched; it is only experienced at the exact moment that it is created, and it has the amazing potential to communicate the mysterious and unknown aspects of God. Like faith, music has the ability to mystify and penetrate the soul in unexplainable ways.

Therefore, music is maybe the most powerful tool in aiding the presence of the Spirit in worship. The music does this with its aural power and by how we associate the sounds and feelings of worship. This can go one of two ways: the music moves heaven into our hearts or it moves our minds towards other things. For music to transcend our heart, it does this through the mind. And if the mind hears sounds that are associated with the world, our hearts are tainted by the worldly influences we hear. Likewise, if heaven moves into our minds through music that is unique to *sacred* associations, are we not sparing our hearts the burden of being tainted by influences other than the Holy Spirit?

---

29. Calvin, *Hebrews*, 27.

30. Man, *Proclamation and Praise*, 75.

Ultimately, in our day where music is readily available and present in every aspect of life, we now have the unprecedented ability as humans to associate the sound of music with any almost given topic.

Bluegrass . . . Appalachian Mountains

I'd Like to Teach the World to Sing . . . Coke

Jazz . . . New Orleans

Sweet Georgia Brown . . . Harlem Globetrotters

Hail to the chief . . . President of the USA

Gershwin Rhapsody in Blue . . . American Airlines

O Happy Day . . . Gospel

For All the Saints (Sine Nomine) . . . heaven

Of course, there is not one specific theme song for heaven, and we could all come up with what we believe to be one, as I have with "For All the Saints." However, there is a sound—an association—that we will conform in our minds to most all music. The scope is broad, but the intent of the music will be very clear for the musician and the listener, and especially to God. It is the duty of the church musician to be aware of how the music shapes the worship service, how it presents the gospel, and most importantly what we are saying about our Savior and our eternal home.

CHAPTER 12

Pragmatism in Church Music

A church fed on excitement is no New Testament church at all. The desire for surface stimulation is a sure mark of the fallen nature, the very thing Christ died to deliver us from. A curious crowd of baptized wordings waiting each Sunday for the quasi-religious needle to give them a lift bears no relation whatsoever to a true assembly of Christian believers.

—A. W. TOZER

IF WE BELIEVE THAT worship is the first priority of the Christian and of the church,[1] congregations should seek to conduct corporate worship in the best possible manner and to believe in the beauty and power of each component. It should be somewhat black and white when we believe that worship is the center of the Christian experience and that we direct our worship only to God and we believe that he deserves our highest standards. Clearly, worship has biblical guidelines and, though there are implications throughout the Bible of how worship should be done, we must therefore consider the implications and end result of the music as much as the practical approach. Unfortunately, the church is infiltrated with political nuances and many other external factors that have dictated the direction for the corporate gathering of covenant believers, especially those concerning music. The pragmatic decisions the church has made over the centu-

1. Westminster Shorter Catechism, question 1 "What is man's chief end? Man's chief end is to glorify and enjoy Him forever."

ries are being demonstrated in the diversity of faiths and the traditions each has established.

C. S. Lewis speaks directly on how pragmatism determines music practice in churches:

> There are two musical situations on which I think we can be confident that a blessing rests. One is where a priest or an organist, himself a man of trained and delicate taste, humbly and charitably sacrifices his own (aesthetically right) desires and gives the people humbler and coarser fare than he would wish, in a belief (even, as it may be, the erroneous belief) that he can thus bring them to God. The other is where the stupid and unmusical layman humbly and patiently, and above all silently, listens to music which he cannot, or cannot fully, appreciate, in the belief that it somehow glorifies God, and that if it does not edify him this must be his own defect. Neither such a High Brow nor such a Low Brow can be far out of the way. To both, Church Music will have been a means of grace; not the music they have liked, but the music they have disliked. They have both offered, sacrificed, their taste in the fullest sense. But where the opposite situation arises, where the musician is filled with the pride of skill or the virus of emulation and looks with contempt on the unappreciative congregation, or where the unmusical, complacently entrenched in their own ignorance and conservatism, look with the restless and resentful hostility of an inferiority complex on all who would try to improve their taste – there, we may be sure, all that both offer is unblessed and the spirit that moves them is not the Holy Ghost.[2]

A Vision of Unified Church Music

A unified vision of corporate worship must be biblically based, nuanced by the past of both individuals and of the church—the two becoming one and manifested in the life of the church. When we speak of the fundamentals, philosophy, and interpretation of worship, we should be thinking with heaven in mind. Though there are overall biblical and theological grounds for all worship, each individual church must keep in mind the unique historical journey, her resources, and identity as a unique body when making decisions on worship. A vision of heavenly worship is not about making a radical change because of a personal belief or a desire for greater earthly

2. Lewis, "On Church Music," para. 1–2.

benefits, but because each church feels a *unique calling and identity based on what has been said is the church's overarching understanding of worship.* However, much of the thinking in the church has been influenced by culture, trends, and media influences over the past century. Tozer speaks on the "symptom of entertainment" as a gross injustice to worship.

> This is the cause of a very serious breakdown in modern evangelicalism. The idea of cultivation and exercise, so dear to the saints of old, has now no place in our total religious picture. It is too slow, too common. We now demand glamour and fast flowing dramatic action. A generation of Christians reared among push buttons and automatic machines is impatient of slower and less direct methods of reaching their goals. We have been trying to apply machine-age methods to our relations with God. We read our chapter, have our short devotions and rush away, hoping to make up for our deep inward bankruptcy by attending another gospel meeting or listening to another thrilling story told by a religious adventurer lately returned from afar. The tragic results of this spirit are all about us: shallow loves, hollow religious philosophies, the preponderance of the element of fun in gospel meetings, the glorification of men, trust in religious externalities, quasi-religious fellowships, salesmanship methods, the mistaking of dynamic personality for the power of the Spirit. These and such as these are the symptoms of an evil disease, a deep and serious malady of the soul.[3]

Recent history proves that matters of worship have been one of potentially keeping the church unified.

> If we identify a feeling as an encounter with God, and only a particular kind of music produces that feeling, then we will insist that same music be played regularly in our church or gatherings. As long as everyone else shares our taste then there is no problem. But if others depend upon a different kind of music to produce the feeling that is important to them then division is cultivated. And because we routinely classify particular feelings as encounters with God our demands for what produce those feelings become very rigid. This is why so many churches succumb to offering multiple styles of worship services. By doing so, they unwittingly sanction division and self-centeredness among the people of God.[4]

3. Tozer, *The Pursuit of God*, 62–63.
4. Pruitt, "Is Your Church Worship Pagan or Christian?" para 9.

Churches have created various options for how to worship as God's people. What do we collectively communicate about God with the variety among different churches, and even more within in a single church? Any stated view of worship obviously can be interpreted in many ways in terms of practical application. When we understand a biblical philosophy and then look at the twenty-first-century church, we can quickly see the potential ways differing approaches to corporate worship can create not only internal differences, but a misconstrued and noncommittal approach to experiencing God in worship. Paul speaks of the church's mixed messages:

> So if the whole church comes together and everyone speaks in tongues, and some who do not understand or some unbelievers come in, will they not say that you are out of your mind? But if an unbeliever or someone who does not understand comes in while everybody is prophesying, he will be convinced by all that he is a sinner and will be judged by all, and the secrets of his heart will be laid bare. So he will fall down and worship God, exclaiming, "God is really among you!"[5]

My own personal experience and testimony to this is the joy and satisfaction of attending a worship service that presents solid liturgy and music that differs from the world of popular trends contrasted with a service that tries to imitate the world. I leave more confused about God's presence and his attributes more than when I first arrived to worship. Should our worship not inspire and inform us and help us to better experience the fullness of the Godhead? For me the question of how to experience a heavenly encounter while being so entrapped by the familiar clothing of the world is ever growing. I have deep concern about how the contrasting views of worship and music will continue to coexist without diminishing the value of the other, especially music and worship elements that are biblically and historical inspiring.

Worship should not be based on personal preferences but a biblical, historical, theological, and experiential approach. Our ongoing Christian discipleship also demands greater attention because our spiritual journey has demanded more of us and what we expect corporate worship to be. The beauty of corporate worship is the joy we embrace from experiencing God apart from the world along with other like-minded Christians. The argument of musical preference as a choice for worship is based on commercialized pop culture and church trends, and lacks understanding about

5. 1 Cor 14:23–25.

the history of church music. It also lacks the ability and desire to experience God in a transcendent way and a perceived lack of desire for growth toward something greater.

To say that we should embrace all expressions of corporate worship is a possible contradiction if we, as a church whole, have any true understanding of worship, the church, and God. If our church leaders have no strong convictions about how we lead our people into the presence of God, or likewise embrace many contrasting philosophies, are we serving some other motives and not trying to give God our undivided best? This approach is possibly pragmatic, promotes narcissism, lacks biblical vision, lacks display of a disciplined Christian life, and is aimed more at the preference rather than desire for Christian unity. If we allow differences to fester for the sake of promoting unity in the present, we will undermine real unity for the future. This unity should look at the future, not just the present. If we as a church continue to allow fundamental differences on issues of worship for the sake of unity, the cycle will continue to escalate. The church will have failed in serving our current generation if we do not hold to a unified belief on what is godly, biblical worship.

If church leaders strive to serve the church as it is, not the people we want in the church, on matters of worship, we should look at whom we are dealing. The twenty-first-century Christian is far more unified, sophisticated, spiritually aware, and more intellectually challenged than most leaders making decisions for the church. I mean this statement as a whole—not the individual work of many great church leaders who are focused on Christ more than the desired results of their ministries. Our culture's consensus style of peer influence by nature compromises, lowers the bar, and settles for overall mediocrity when we make decisions on worship for the church—all for the sake of unity. Each church should feel called to serve the gospel and bring it to life with all the resources God has given it more than compromising important matters for the sake of trying to make everyone equally happy, especially when deciding what music is appropriate for corporate worship.

Many discussions are taking place among pastors and church musicians as to the role of music in the church and its desired result for that church. Calvin Johannasen, says, "the pragmatist does not judge music itself to be either good or bad. It's worth lies totally in its ability to bring the results assigned to it . . .

The pragmatist, in the name of communication, emasculates the gospel by using commercialized music to sell it. The gospel is stripped of its full integrity and power, and manipulative marketing techniques supplant the work of the Spirit.[6]

The pragmatic decisions that often shape church music and worship are based on many factors. Everett Ferguson points out four common misunderstandings of worship, (which can be deduced all as pragmatic):

an external or mechanical interpretation of worship
an individualistic interpretation
an emotional uplift interpretation; and
a performance interpretation.[7]

Paul Jones also speaks of the value system that the postmodern church has taken on that reflects our society's primary philosophy (what "works"— *pragmatism*), its object of attention (ourselves—*narcissism*), its occupation (our own amusement or pleasure—*hedonism*), and its basis of beliefs (our opinions—*relativism*).[8]

As identified, there are many issues of pragmatism that are shaping the present church and her music. Though we cannot go through all of these brought forth above, I would like to identify some of the pragmatic issues that are the current threads of ideas being formulated to shape current church music.

Matters of the Heart and the World:
Why We Should Look Up

It is very sad to hear some Christians say that they cannot understand or "get" some aspects or forms of worship. Many deduce that with formal and stuffy churches they don't experience God the same way they do at less formal worship services. This is a serious contradiction to the heart of Christian worship and discipleship. To offer worship that is geared to mimic the sound and ways of the world is completely missing the point of God's presence in the worship.[9] The job of the church is to teach these

---

6. Johansson, *Music and Ministry*, 29.

7. Ferguson, *The Church of Christ*, 227–29.

8. Jones, *Singing and Making Music*, 188.

9. 1 John 2:15–17; 1 Cor 2:12; Jas 4:4.

PRAGMATISM IN CHURCH MUSIC

biblical principles. Jeffrey Meyers tells of an experience on his realization of the importance of teaching his flock how to worship:[10]

> I have often called on visitors who were not raised in the church, any church. I recall one recent case. She was what some would call a "seeker," someone looking for a church. During my visitation she told me that she was having a difficult time with our liturgy. She had attended our worship service twice. "It takes a lot of work to know where we are and why we are doing what we are doing," she confided. I was about to "apologize" for our worship and encourage her, when she made a remarkable confession. She said, "You know, Pastor, I realize that I am a very new Christian. I know that I don't know my Bible. I don't know very many of the hymns that you sing. The music is not familiar to me, since I didn't grow up in a church. But that doesn't bother me, because I also know that I have a lot to learn. I shouldn't expect to know how to worship after two weeks of church, should I? I look at all the children in your church and I weep. They know the hymns. They know where to turn in their Bibles. I want to learn all of that, too. I wasn't raised that way. I need to learn how to worship God. Will you be patient with me and help? It's hard." Now that's only a summary of what she said. It almost made me weep right there on the spot. Tears did come to my eyes in the car driving home. It as not so much that the service was "unintelligible" to her; it was just unfamiliar. She simply had to *learn* how to worship.

The importance of understanding corporate worship (and why we should teach on it) is the only way any of us have learned to worship. Should the corporate worship experience not be the one truly unique time when the *corporate* church gathers to *offer praise in way that we can only do corporately* and in the fashion that God has taught us to approach him?

Every biblical description of worship demonstrates a dynamic that is a high and regal affair. Nothing like the informal, comfy approach that we think the fallen people of the world want. Instead of shirking the beautiful task of teaching the importance of the *higher* way, let us call for Christians to worship with deeper meaning, understanding, and most certainly be reminded of the heavenly worship we will enjoy in God's almighty presence. God is the only factor in matters of heart and worship. If we look to the world for the answers, we will be sorely disappointed.

---

10. Meyers, *The Lord's Service*, 209.

There are those who are more influenced by the world than by the New Testament, and they are not ready for the Holy Spirit. Of these people, we have to say that they are influenced far more by Hollywood than they are by Jerusalem. Their spirit and mode of life is more like Hollywood than it is like Jerusalem. If you were to suddenly set them down in the New Jerusalem, they would not feel at home because their mode, the texture of their mind, has been created for them by twentieth century entertainment and not by the things of God.[11]

Further, we must consider the intent of our music in church. If our goal is to demonstrate our talent, our show of our wonderful instruments, we have missed the heavenly intent of leading God's people in worship. C. S. Lewis speaks sharply on this point:

It seems to me that we must define rather carefully the way, or ways, in which music can glorify God. There is . . . a sense in which all natural agents, even inanimate ones, glorify God continually by revealing the powers He has given them. And in that sense we, as natural agents, do the same. On that level our wicked actions, in so far as they exhibit our skill and strength, may be said to glorify God, as well as our good actions. An excellently performed piece of music, as natural operation which reveals in a very high degree the peculiar powers given to man, will thus always glorify God whatever the intention of the performers may be. But that is a kind of glorifying which we share with the "dragons and great deeps", with the "frost and snows". What is looked for in us, as men, is another kind of glorifying, which depends on intention. How easy or how hard it may be for a whole choir to preserve that intention through all the discussions and decisions, all the corrections and the disappointments, all the temptations to pride, rivalry and ambition, which precede the performance of a great work, I (naturally) do not know. But it is on the intention that all depends. When it succeeds, I think the performers are the most enviable of men; privileged while mortals to honor God like angels and, for a few golden moments, to see spirit and flesh, delight and labour, skill and worship, the natural and the supernatural, all fused into that unity they would have had before the Fall.[12]

Though we are laboring over the expectation of heaven, and striving to work with the best musical forms the world has developed thus far, the

11. Tozer, *Tozer on Worship*, 168.

12. Lewis, "On Church Music," 135.

far more important matter is the sentiment that Charles Spurgeon shares with his congregation in a sermon on "heavenly worship:"

> You must learn to feel that "sweeter sounds than music knows mingle in your Savior's name," or else you can never chant the hallelujahs of the blest before the throne of the great "I AM." Take that thought, whatever else you forget; treasure it up in your memory, and ask by the grace of God that you may here be taught to sing the heavenly song, that afterwards in the land of the hereafter, in the home of the beautified, you may continually chant the high praises of him that loved you.[13]

Evangelism

In a recent conversation with a church youth director, I experienced pragmatism being used under the guise of evangelism. The discussion was centered around why we should use music being produced from the contemporary genre, even if we feel it will not have a long shelf life in our churches. The justification from the youth leader is that if it is working at the moment, it is serving its purpose and therefore serving the kingdom of God.

Worship must be first priority, even over evangelism. This may be a new concept to our modern church thinkers. Perhaps the hallmark of why our worship patterns have changed so dramatically has been based on the premise of evangelism. This trend has been the model of most megachurch worship services and many studies and much research has been done to either reconcile or squash the marriage of worship as evangelism. The claim of offering a more friendly approach to worship or church music as outreach seems to be the "tail wagging the dog" approach to ministry. Lee Strobel says in a study of the Willow Creek congregation that the church deliberately set out to make church music different because their research showed, "the number-one reason previously unchurched baby boomers give as to why they come to church is: 'They play my music.' It is perhaps true that the majority of unchurched seekers, as compared to the church-reared subjects of their study do prefer contemporary music because it is popularized in mass culture."[14] If we lose focus of worship doctrine, how

13. Spurgeon, "Heavenly Worship," part II, para. 8.
14. Strobel, *Inside the Mind*, 180.

can we expect to evangelize the world about the high and omnipotent God we serve?

> The feeling that we've got to make converts at any cost has greatly wounded the Church of Christ. We must present the truth as we are told to present it and let the Holy Ghost work . . . this soft idea in order to keep people coming and giving and filling the seats we don't dare in any wise offend them, and we've got to make everything smooth and soft, is not New Testament.[15]

From the opposite spectrum, corporate worship can be an excellent form of evangelism. In fact, worship can be one of the most transforming events in the salvation of a non-believer who experiences the richness of God's unhindered presence among corporate worshippers. However, the key to this model is the importance of displaying a vivid portrayal of a Christian life being sincerely shaped by worship, and not just a cultural imitation of the kind of false gods that society embraces which are mimicked in the midst of a seemingly familiar environment created by the external factors that churches like to market church services with.

> For centuries the church stood solidly against every form of worldly entertainment, recognizing it for what it was—a device for wasting time, a refuge from the disturbing voice of conscience, a scheme to divert attention from moral accountability. For this she got herself abused roundly by the sons of this world. But of late she has become tired of the abuse and has given over the struggle. She appears to have decided that if she cannot conquer the great god Entertainment she may as well join forces with him and make what use she can of his powers. So today we have the astonishing spectacle of millions of dollars being poured into the unholy job of providing earthly entertainment for the so-called sons of heaven. Religious entertainment is in many places rapidly crowding out the serious things of God. Many churches these days have become little more than poor theaters where fifth-rate "producers" peddle their shoddy wares with the full approval of evangelical leaders who can even quote a holy text in defense of their delinquency. And hardly a man dares raise his voice against it.[16]

Worship should not be aimed at the least common denominator, but the opposite. Likewise, the gospel should not seem out of reach to the

---

15. Tozer, *Tozer on Worship*, 141–42.
16. Tozer, *The Root of the Righteous*, 32–33.

seeker or the new or stagnant Christian. But, the worship and liturgy of mature Christians should display a high priority of walking faithfully in the gospel. Christian worship, when filled with rich teaching, hymnody, and Scripture, can make the faith actually seem more true to the seeker who may not completely understand everything going on, but is often intrigued by the unfamiliarity. This concept especially reinforces relational ministry. When the friends of seekers who are deeply involved in the life of corporate worship are faithful to worship, the seeker friend will often be influenced by that testimony more than anything else, especially overhyped worship elements. This seems to be a more natural approach to evangelism associated with worship.

The worship service must remain focused on God with elements designed to aid current followers of Christ into closer communion and fellowship with him and one another. Retooling worship services and its elements to simply have appeal to the lost may be noble, but is not to whom or to what godly worship should be aimed.

> While we are generally careful not to say so, there seems to be a tendency to treat worship as something which is for us. Don't misunderstand. There are great blessings to be had in worshipping God. What is more, God does not require our worship as though he needs something from us (Acts 17:22–25). Rather, God calls us to worship him because of His essential worthiness. God demanded the release of his people from Egypt that they might worship Him (Ex 5:1). The Psalms repeatedly call upon the people of God to worship the Lord because of who he is and what he has done. We worship God because it is always right for the creature to worship the Creator.[17]

This context for evangelism has, perhaps unknowingly, made a dramatic impact in Christian circles by cheapening the gospel and the relationship with God and his covenant children. In our zeal for evangelism, we should not forget that no matter how the worship is structured, or which style of music is used, the Holy Spirit ultimately completes the work.

> Listen, brethren, we can become promoters and get nowhere at all. But if we become prophets and worshipers of God, God will honor us in this awful hour in which we live. I think we ought to go to our churches and insist that we adore God.

---

17. Pruitt, "Is Your Worship Pagan or Christian?" para 7.

And if we can't adore him, we ought to get purged from our sins until we can.[18]

Lastly, corporate worship should not compromise "excellence" for the sake of evangelism. Perhaps this is the most understood concept among the pragmatist whose criteria is based on "what works now." Just as the youth leader could place value in certain pieces of music that he felt would not stand the test of time, it is the job of the church and the church musician to help maintain the standard of excellence in worship.

Second Peter 1:3 speaks of how our knowledge and lifestyles should seek the excellence of Christ's glory:

> His divine power has granted to us all things that pertain to life and godliness, through the knowledge of him who called us to his own glory and excellence . . .

Relevance

I can safely say, on the authority of all that is revealed in the Word of God, that any man or woman on this earth who is bored and turned off by worship is not ready for heaven.

—A. W. TOZER[19]

Perhaps the most frequently used buzzword of disgruntled and unhappy worshippers is relevance. Those who lead and begin new models of worship almost always want to develop a new approach to church worship as a response to their own personal claim that their worship experience has not been relevant to them. The stories of stodgy preachers, old ladies playing the organ, and hymns they can't understand and don't know what they mean are the most common reasons Christians feel led away from the now former mode of common worship trends. Perhaps this is true. Many have seen cases of impassionate and what appears to be uninspired worship. Often times, church worship is completely misunderstood because of the lack of commercialized traits that unchurched seekers may expect. Likewise, the "excitement" of worship or the music presented does not match the level of what a televised church service may convey. Does this mean that Christians

18. Tozer, *Tozer on Worship*, 142–43.

19. Ibid., 34.

in less developed parts of the world, such as Africa or even the small countryside church, are worshipping God any less than those who have highly developed forms of worship?

So, what is relevance? The word *relevant*, by definition "implies a traceable, significant or logical connection to the matter at hand." While worship should be completely relevant to all who sincerely believe in Christ and the work of the Holy Spirit within the church, the question can be raised as to why any aspect of Christ's work would not be relevant to any of his followers. What makes worship relevant to worshippers? Content or presentation? The question I raise is: does the presentation change the content (the logical connection to the matter at hand)? Does our desire to have so-called more relevant music and worship practices altered for the sake of *relevance* have any weight in actually communicating the gospel message? Again, is this not the work of God alone?

The church should always be *reforming* and evaluating how *relevant* we are in our ministries—not how relevant we are to the culture, and not to simply mirror every change the culture makes. The changes that the church makes should be at a healthy pace that can be easily accepted by the church at the given time. We should not fancy ourselves as dictating the trends and being ahead of the curve, but that we healthily evaluate the effectiveness before jumping onboard with the newest and latest *culturally relevant* practices.

The same is applicable in the pace of reforming the church's music. We should evaluate the staying power of the good music and then incorporate it appropriately into our repertoire of congregational song. In most churches, we have healthily done this with the addition of some excellent hymns such as "In Christ Alone" and "How Deep the Father's Love for Us" to our repertoire. The church did this in the 1950s with "How Great Thou Art" and "Great Is Thy Faithfulness." Though the popular gospel song "Turn Your Radio On" was popular at the same time, it did not make it to the church's repertoire of standard hymns. These songs demonstrated their staying power, their ability to lead all in worship with no single generational appeal, because they equally appeal to all ages; a sign of good *corporate worship* music. The high quality of these new songs is demonstrated in their ability to be presented in any context, musically and liturgically.

In contrast, the changing pace of contemporary music creates a constant need for updating and coming up with new songs. In looking at the song selections from our contemporary service over the past fifteen years in five-year intervals, I can clearly deduce that the most popular songs, based on frequency of use within the service, are now obsolete and would be considered "lame" by the people we claim to try to reach. Example: "He Is Exalted," 1985, first introduced in 1992 at our church, last used in 2004; "Lord, I Lift Your Name on High," 1989, first introduced in 1992, last used in 2009. The songs that have been consistent across fifteen years of worship are "Be Thou My Vision," "Come, Thou Fount of Every Blessing," "All Creatures of Our God and King," and so on. All hymns whose texts are over 250 years old, and whose music is almost the same have proven the test of time.

However, some of the trends in contemporary songs are demonstrating differences from former styles of songs written for congregational singing that I would like to point out here:

1. Theological soundness. Some of these songs have strong overtones of narcissism, and are generally inconsistent with the biblical themes of majesty and royal approach to the throne of God.

> Religious music has long ago fallen victim to this weak and twisted philosophy of godliness. Good hymnody has been betrayed and subverted by noisy, uncouth persons who have too long operated under the immunity afforded them by the timidity of the saints. The tragic result is that for one entire generation we have been rearing Christians who are in complete ignorance of the golden treasury of songs and hymns left us by the ages. It is ironic that the modernistic churches which deny the theology of the great hymns nevertheless sing them, and regenerated Christians who believe them are yet not singing them; in their stead are songs without theological content set to music without beauty. Not our religious literature only and our hymnody have suffered from the notion that love to be true to itself must be silent in the presence of any and every abomination, but almost every phase of our church life has suffered also.[20]

2. Repetition. The culture of the contemporary song movement leads to cycles of overly emotional repetition driven by the music. *But when ye pray, use not vain repetitions, as the heathen do: for they think that they shall be heard for their much speaking.*[21] Though this is speaking specifically on prayer, most of our songs of praise to God can be deduced to forms of prayer, so therefore, I question the validity of these pat-

---

20. Tozer, *The Size of the Soul*, 189–90.

21. Matt 6:7.

terns. This type of repetition creates an overly emotional response not based on the truth of the gospel. This is the vain repetition expressed in Matthew 6:7. The difference between repetition in contemporary worship and that used in historic liturgies is that the latter has the goal of instilling biblical truth deep into our souls. It is designed to shape us into the image of Christ over the course of one's life. The repetition of doctrine is transformation in our learning and embedding of sentiment, while some of the repetitiveness of contemporary genre is a more broadly emotional expression on behalf of the individual worshipper, not the congregation as a whole.

3. Charismatic tendencies. Much of the music broadcast on Christian music radio stations is heavily influenced by charismatic-based ministries. While personal expressions of worship are between the Lord and the one offering the praise, the effects of peer-pressured expression in the corporate setting raise questions of authenticity. The trend of the contemporary Christian music scene is built on a sea of individuals worshipping in their own realm of expression, much of which has now become expectation among those worshipping together in such a context. One particular evaluation is how the emotion, or climax of the music, almost always idiomatically produces the simultaneous raising of hands among these groups. It is as if the music itself indicates the place and time to engage in hand raising and/or eye closing. Seemingly, the music dictates the expression, rather than the expression being a spontaneous act of praise from the worshipper.

4. Contextualization. Music that is so similar to popular music generally does not lead to "heavenly" worship. Because the music sounds just like the popular secular artists, the people who listen to this music are drawn into their comfort zone, instead of being taken out of it—into the "upper room" of the Lord, or into his heavenly presence.

Lastly, we should not assume that change in the church's music is always for the good of all. The church has often made compromise based on the perceived desires of the upcoming younger generations. Robert Wuthnow raises alternative points.

> Journalists have begun to note that the stereotypic picture of generational preferences about worship may not be accurate. Some of the young people journalists interview say the innovative worship styles that appealed to baby boomers do not appeal to them. They think church services should feel

like church. They say the so-called seeker services that were geared toward people who disliked church are now passé. In the major research project I did a few years ago on the uses of music and the arts in congregations, I observed, too, that young adults were often as interested in preserving traditional worship as they were in changing it.[22]

22. Wuthnow, *After the Baby Boomers*, 290.

CHAPTER 13

In the Image of God

God created man in His own image,
in the image of God He created him.
—GENESIS 1:27

WE ARE CREATED IN the image of God. "Moreover, since the glory of God ought, in a measure, to shine in the several parts of our bodies, it is especially fitting that the tongue has been assigned and destined for this task, both through singing and through speaking. For it was peculiarly created to tell and proclaim the praise of God."[1] In other words, singing the praises of God is part of man's task in carrying out the moral perfection involved in the *imago Dei*.

The doctrine of *imago Dei* was first introduced to me through the writing of Dorothy Sayers, who speaks on the parallel in Genesis to God's creating and ours:

> We are told in Genesis 1:26 that the Creator proposes to make man in His own "image and likeness." There has been much speculation about what might be the meaning or content of this likeness. On the basis of the text itself, we may observe that up to this point in the narrative, the reader has been told only one thing about God that would enable him to attach some content to the notion of the likeness to God. He has been told of God's activity as the Creator. One might therefore justly conclude that the meaning of the image

1. Calvin, *Institutes*, 3.20.31.

and likeness—or at least one meaning of it—is that man shall be like God in his creativity. Be creative as your Father in heaven is creative.[2]

This doctrine or theology of creating in the image of God has been agreed upon among many classical Christian thinkers as a gift to the human race. The history of the doctrine of the *imago Dei* demonstrates how theologians adapted their understanding in light of prevailing philosophies of the day. James Leo Garrett states, "some theologians have opted not for a single view of the image but for a composite of selected views, but normally they have done little toward the integration of the views placed in the composite."[3] The substantive approach details the characteristic ways in which humanity mirrors God, but because of its reliance on the Old Testament texts, it fails to address the triune nature of the God whom humanity images. Much historical evidence supports the understanding of the image as a function, yet it fails to address the New Testament ideas of a loving response and characterization of God. The relational approach logically addresses many of the philosophical questions regarding the image and society, but falters due to a lack of a clear biblical foundation.

The imago as the divine calling and profession embodies elements of each perspective but identifies the primary aspect of biblical anthropology to be a lifestyle of worship that reflects the glory of the Creator and lovingly relates to the rest of creation. Jeremy Begbie describes this dynamic:

> Understandably then, some refer to human beings as "priests of creation." The phrase is apt, for it speaks of a double movement. On behalf of God, as God's image bearers, humans are to mediate the presence of God to the world and in the world, representing his wise and loving rule. But this is so that on behalf of creation humans may gather and focus creation's worship, offering it back to God, voicing creation's praise.[4]

Likewise, the exercise of the creative gifts bestowed to humanity by its Creator reflects his glory throughout the world. The structuralist viewpoint of the *imago Dei* teaches that humanity shares certain communicable attributes or capabilities with the Creator, albeit on a far different scale and level of quality. Society long has recognized the arts as a "spark of the divine" and

2. Sayers, *The Mind of the Maker*, 22.

3. Garrett, *Systematic Theology*, 462.

4. Begbie, *Resounding Truth*, 203.

one of the most important distinguishing characteristics of humanity. The exercise of dominion over music, art, dance, and language, for example, fulfills the creation directive to subdue the earth. Calvin Johannson connects this exercise of dominion with the *imago Dei*:

> We have said that in the creation mandate everyone, regenerate or not, is given the responsibility to assist in God's ongoing creation, *creatio continua*. We are endowed with the tools for this task via the broad sense of the *imago Dei*, and create because it is part of our nature. Further, in the narrow sense of the *imago Dei*, Christians face the prospect that through their actions (including their music) God is made known. Church music is testimony, and in worship believers use cultural expressions, such as music, to show what God has done, what he means, and who he is.[5]

To be the image of God means to display the glory of God and proclaim his kingdom on the earth. We are to serve as mirrors in which God can reflect the surpassing worth of his nature to the entire creation. Worship is not about us at all; it is supremely focused upon the Father, Son, and Spirit and his work of redemption. In *Engaging with God*, David Peterson says, "The whole point of creation is that God should have a reflection in which he reflects himself and in which the image of God as the Creator is revealed, so that through it God is attested, confirmed and proclaimed."[6]

John Piper echoes this calling of worship:

> But since God made man like himself, man's dominion over the world and his filling the world is a display—an imaging forth—of God. God's aim, therefore, was that man would so act that he mirror forth God, who has ultimate dominion. Man is given the exalted status as image-bearer not so he would become arrogant and autonomous (as he tried to do in the Fall), but so he would reflect the glory of His Maker whose image he bears. God's purpose in creation, therefore, was to fill the earth with his own glory.[7]

To image God is to worship him, as the redeemed image bearer conforms to the original *imago Dei* and reflects the Trinity in his or her sphere of relationships. The *imago Dei* is the calling to reflect the glory of God and the enactment of this reality upon the earth. While it will always be necessary to contend for the truth of the faith, it will be the image bearers

---

5. Johansson, *Music and Ministry*, 36.

6. Peterson, *Engaging With God*, 170.

7. Piper, *Desiring God*, 256.

whose lives most clearly reflect the glory of God, extend his kingdom into this world, and have the most impact on the postmodern society. Fulfilling the destiny of the *imago Dei*, redeemed believers tell the grand story of God's plan from before the foundation of the world and proclaim to a world devoid of meaning and hope that true identity can be found in relationship with the Creator. The questions of identity and self-actualization can only be answered in a responsible loving relationship between man and his Creator. An individual finds true meaning only as he or she serves as a mirror in which the glory of God is displayed. As the worshipper magnifies the triune God, celebrates his magnificent story of redemption, and lives as a sign of the kingdom to come, then he or she truly becomes *imago Dei*.[8]

Truly, creating in the "image of God" is the call of the musician in the church who facilitates the church's praise into the courts of heaven, so that the glory of God is revealed on earth. The implication for the church musician is to consider the grand privilege of selecting and presenting music in the church for the glory of Christ's kingdom on "earth, as it is heaven."

> God the Creator as shown forth by the church musician's music is often a frightening prospect! We image God in the music we do. When the program is hit-or-miss, we show forth a God who lacks purpose and direction; when our work is not well prepared, we image a God who is lazy and slothful; when the performance preparation is a last-minute affair, we show forth a procrastinating God; when our performance of music lacks vitality or artistic grace, we show God to be inert; when our musical choices revolve around our favorite style or body of composition, God is seen as rigid and unbending; and, above all, when the music we choose lacks creativity in the fullest sense (to break new ground imaginatively and with integrity), we image forth a God of "creative" mediocrity . . . The question each church musician faces is not, "Shall I?" but, "What will be the image set forth?"[9]

8. Toledo, "Created in God's Image," 13–15.
9. Johansson, *Music and Ministry*, 28–29.

CHAPTER 14

Worship that Looks Up: A Heavenward Approach to Church Music

Glory now to Thee be given,
On earth as in the highest heaven.
With lute and harp in sweetest tone.

All of pearl each dazzling portal,
Where we shall join the song immortal,
Of Saints and Angels round Thy throne.

Beyond all earthly ken
Those wondrous joys remain,
That God prepares.
Our hearts rejoice, i-o! i-o!
Ever in dulci jubilo!

—FROM LUTHERAN CHORALE, "WACHET AUF";
PHILIPP NICOLAI, 1599

From earth's wide bounds, from ocean's farthest coast,
Through gates of pearl streams in the countless host,
And singing to Father, Son and Holy Ghost: Alleluia, Alleluia!

—FINAL VERSE OF "FOR ALL THE SAINTS"; WILLIAM HOW, 1864

A. W. Tozer speaks of the *Incredible Christian* and the anticipation of heaven that is not understood by the world, and especially, "He cheerfully expects before long to enter that bright world above, but is in no hurry to leave this world and is quite willing to await the summons of his Heavenly Father. And he is unable to understand why the critical unbeliever should condemn him for this: it all seems so natural and right in the circumstances that he sees nothing inconsistent about it."[1]

The challenges within church music will continue to be in how we contend with the changing and influential power of our worldly and "pop" driven surroundings—those who do understand the Christian hope of heaven and how we celebrate that hope through the mystery of the table—liturgy—worship. There are some ways which secular society sees royalty and majesty. For example, the rich tradition of the British monarchs and many other royal families have set an earthly expectation of how we approach the earthly royalty. The traditions established by the collective practices of past and present generations of royalty give us an example of our earthly ability to set a high bar for a rich and regal showing of pomp and ceremony.

Just looking at a few of the royal psalms, we see the kingly reign of our Lord, displayed in Scripture, with all the associations of royalty. Psalm 2, for instance, speaks of the king's reign:

> Why do the nations rage
> and the peoples plot in vain?
> The kings of the earth set themselves,
> and the rulers take counsel together,
> against the Lord and against his Anointed, saying,
> "Let us burst their bonds apart
> and cast away their cords from us."
>
> He who sits in the heavens laughs;
> the Lord holds them in derision.
> Then he will speak to them in his wrath,
> and terrify them in his fury, saying,
> "As for me, I have set my King
> on Zion, my holy hill."
>
> I will tell of the decree:
> The Lord said to me, "You are my Son;

---

1. Tozer, *The Incredible Christian*, 41.

today I have begotten you.
Ask of me, and I will make the nations your heritage,
and the ends of the earth your possession.
You shall break them with a rod of iron
and dash them in pieces like a potter's vessel."

Now therefore, O kings, be wise;
be warned, O rulers of the earth.
Serve the Lord with fear,
and rejoice with trembling.
Kiss the Son,
lest he be angry, and you perish in the way,
for his wrath is quickly kindled.
Blessed are all who take refuge in him.

Our Lord is King over all, and as Scripture has said here—will have decree over all the kings of the earth. These verses certainly put the reign of God over earthly princes in perspective, yet we still tend to give pageantry to earthly rituals than to that which God has so clearly prescribed his children to give to him while on earth. How do we Christians carry out the heavenly vision of life and worship? Tozer summarizes the Christian life as if in heaven—all the issues addressed in this book on Christian leadership carried out in the music of the church: grace, beauty, love, humility, mystery, joy, awe, reverence, paradox and countercultural life and ministry.

> The Christian believes that in Christ he has died, yet he is more alive than before and he fully expects to live forever. He walks on earth while seated in heaven and though born on earth he finds that after his conversion, he is not at home here. Like the nighthawk, which in the air is the essence of grace and beauty, but on the ground is awkward and ugly, so the Christian appears at his best in the heavenly places, but does not fit well into the ways of the very society into which he was born. The Christian soon learns that if he would be victorious as a son of heaven among men on earth he must not follow the common pattern of mankind, but rather the contrary. That he may be safe he puts himself in jeopardy, he loses his life to save it and is in danger of losing it if he attempts to preserve it. He goes down to get up. If he refuses to go down he is already down, but when he starts down he is on his way up.
>
> He is strongest when he is weakest and weakest when he is strong. Though poor he has the power to make others rich, but when he becomes rich his ability to enrich others vanishes. He

has the most after he has given most away and has least when he possesses most.

He may be and often is highest when he feels lowest and most sinless when he is most conscious of sin. He is wisest when he knows that he knows not and knows least when he has acquired the greatest amount of knowledge. He sometimes does most by doing nothing and goes furthest when standing still. In heaviness he manages to rejoice and keeps his heart glad even in sorrow.

The paradoxical character of the Christian is revealed constantly. For instance, he believes that he is saved now, nevertheless he expects to be saved later and looks forward joyfully to future salvation. He fears God but is not afraid of Him. In God's presence he feels overwhelmed and undone yet there is nowhere he would rather be than in that presence. He knows that he has been cleansed from his sin, yet he is painfully conscious that in his flesh dwells no good thing.

He loves supremely One whom he has never seen, and though himself poor and lowly he talks familiarly with One who is King of all Kings and Lord of all lords and is aware of no incongruity in so doing.[2]

2. Ibid., 62–63.

A Philosophy and Identity for the Corporate Church

*Music is the means of recapturing the original joy
and beauty of Paradise.*

—HILDEGARD VON BINGEN

CHRIST DEFINED HEAVENLY WORSHIP to the Samaritan woman in John 4. When the woman was confronted by Jesus regarding her sin, Christ took the opportunity to address the proper means of worship. "Jesus said to her, 'Woman, believe Me, the hour is coming when you will neither on this mountain, nor in Jerusalem, worship the Father. You worship what you do not know; we know what we worship, for salvation is of the Jews. But the hour is coming, and now is, when the true worshippers will worship the Father in spirit and truth; for the Father is seeking such to worship Him. God is Spirit, and those who worship Him must worship in spirit and truth.'"[1]

Scott Aniol offers a synopsis of this Scripture passage:

> Because of God's strict comments concerning worship, the Jews at that time were very concerned with the outward forms—where, when, and how they should worship. The woman was asking what the proper outward forms of worship should be. Jesus replied that with His coming, the outward forms weren't necessary anymore, and He emphasized the two essential elements of worship, namely spiritual response (spirit) and understanding of truth (truth). Therefore,

1. John 4:21–24.

worship can be defined as follows: Worship is a spiritual response to God as a result of understanding biblical truth about God. This definition captures the biblical essence of worship and can be expressed in countless ways through actions, attitudes, and affections. In reality, worship should encompass all of life . . .[2]

This summary of worship from the mouth of Jesus, is the crux for the church musician in developing a philosophy of music in the church. The importance of the human response to the biblical understanding of God requires a very broad understanding of God and his Word. Through the various Scripture and historical writings about the heavenly view of worship, the high regard for reverence, and the earthly worship that is akin to the attitude of our perception of heaven, we have seen he importance of heavenly worship.

Though the world has many ideas of what makes or constitutes the qualities of good music, the church, likewise, deals with the same broad and varied view of how to best utilize music in our worship. We can study the Bible, historical worship, theology, and the cultural trends and still have ideas as broad as the sea. Ultimately, we will not know what God thinks of our music until we get to heaven. Until that glorious day, we are still left on earth to be challenged by the thought and work of achieving the most highly attainable status of music to be used in the corporate worship of Almighty God.

At the height of an era of creative output and with the centuries of vast contributions made to solidifying the question of what God wills best for his church in matters of music, we seemingly now have more options than ever before. This could be part of the problem—one that probably did not exist until the beginning of the communication age when we gained access to so much material, especially corporate worship music. It would be easy to suspect that the church of the twenty-first century has a far greater repertoire of music than any church in biblical times, even at the height of the Renaissance, which is almost unparalleled with its vast artistic output.

Just as the musician practices his or her instrument alone or rehearses with other musicians, the experience is transformational—development and growth are occurring. Just the definition of the word *practice* implies the actual application or use of an idea, belief, or method as opposed to theories about such application or use *or* repeated exercise in or performance of an activity or skill so as to acquire or maintain proficiency in it.

2. Aninol, *Worship in Song*, 8.

With our earthly worship we are rehearsing for heaven—we are practicing our faith by worshipping with the hope of heaven in mind.

So, with all these options, how do we reconcile our church music, and all the differences we have, with the glorious image of heavenly worship? We can only look up. Church musicians must look to and long for heaven in order to be the artists that God deserves. We must look to heaven when selecting the music, preparing it for worship, and ultimately while leading. Philosophies, cultures, music, styles, and the world changes, but heaven does not. History has proven that even the souls of God's children have not changed. We all long for something greater than the world has to offer, and the worship and music of the church has an ability to take us to a heavenly realm. This is a great task for the church and her leaders. However, the beauty of resting assured that God is glorified through the feeble earthly gifts we offer, for the church's sanctification through Jesus Christ is the reward for being a good and faithful servant.

Bibliography

Aniol, Scott. *Worship in Song: A Biblical Approach to Music and Worship*. Winona Lake, IN: BMH, 2009.

Aune, David E. "The Influence of Roman Imperial Court Ceremonial on the Apocalypse of John." *Biblical Research* 28 (1983) 5–26.

Begbie, Jeremy S. *Resounding Truth: Christian Wisdom in the World of Music*. Grand Rapids: Baker, 2007.

Belcher, Jim. *Deep Church: A Third Way Beyond Emerging and Traditional*. Downers Grove, IL: InterVarsity, 2009.

Bennett, Arthur, ed. *The Valley of Vision: A Collection of Puritan Prayers*. Carlisle, PA: Banner of Truth Trust, 1975.

Best, Harold. *Unceasing Worship: Biblical Perspectives on Worship and the Arts*. Downers Grove, IL: InterVarsity, 2003.

Block, Daniel I. *For the Glory of God: Recovering a Biblical Theology of Worship*. Grand Rapids: Baker, 2014.

Boschman, Lamar. *A Heart For Worship: Experience a Rebirth of Worship*. Lake Mary, FL: Charisma, 1994.

Brother Lawrence. *The Practice of the Presence of God*. New Kensington, PA: Whitaker, 1944.

Brueggemann, Walter. *The Message of the Psalms*. Minneapolis: Augsburg, 1984.

———. *Spirituality of the Psalms*. Minneapolis: Augsburg, 2002.

Caird, G. B. *A Commentary on the Revelation of St. John the Divine*. New York: Harper & Row, 1966.

Calvin, John. *Articles Concerning the Organization of the Church* in *Calvin: Theological Treatises*. Translated by J. K. S. Reid. Philadelphia: Westminster, 1954.

———. *Commentary of John Calvin*. Translated by John King. Grand Rapids: Baker, 1996.

———. *Hebrews and The First and Second Epistles of St. Peter (Calvin's Commentary)*. Translated by W. B. Johnston. Edinburgh: St. Andrew's Press, 1963.

———. *Institutes of the Christian Religion*. Edited by John McNeill. Translated by Ford Lewis Battles. Philadelphia: Westminster, 1960.

Collins, Adela Yarbro. *Crisis and Catharsis: The Power of the Apocalypse*. Philadelphia: Westminster, 1984.

Dyck, John T. "Calvin and Worship." *WRS Journal* 16/1 (February 2009) 33–40.

Farhadian, Charles. *Christian Worship Worldwide: Expanding Horizons, Deepening Practices.* Grand Rapids: Eerdmans, 2007.

Ferguson, Everett. *The Church of Christ: A Biblical Ecclesiology for Today.* Grand Rapids: Eerdmans, 1996.

Furr, Gary A., and Milburn Price. *The Dialogue of Worship: Creating Space for Revelation and Response.* Macon, GA: Smyth & Helwys, 1998.

Gardiner, John Elliot. *Bach: Music in the Castle of Heaven.* New York: Knopf, 2013.

Garrett, James Leo, Jr. *Systematic Theology: Biblical, Historical, and Evangelical.* Vol. 1. 2nd ed. North Richland Hills, TX: Bibal, 2000.

Hart, D. G., and John R. Muether. *With Reverence and Awe: Reclaiming Reformed Worship.* Phillipsburg, NJ: P&R, 2002.

Henry, Matthew. *Matthew Henry's Commentary: In One Volume.* Grand Rapids: Zondervan, 1960.

Hill, Andrew E. *Enter His Courts With Praise: Old Testament Worship for the New Testament Church.* Grand Rapids: Baker, 1993.

Horton, Michael. *A Better Way: Rediscovering the Drama of God-Centered Worship.* Grand Rapids: Baker, 2002.

Jespson, Barbara. "Turning the Guitar Upside Down." *Wall Street Journal*, March 7, 2001. http://www.wsj.com/articles/SB983925616283851571.

Johansson, Calvin. *Music and Ministry: A Biblical Counterpoint.* Peabody, MA: Hendrickson, 1998.

Johnson, Terry. *Leading in Worship: A Sourcebook for Presbyterian Students and Ministers Drawing From the Biblical and Historical Forms of the Reformed Tradition.* Powder Springs, GA: Tolle Lege, 2013.

———. "Worship and Music Today." Independent Presbyterian Church, Savannah, GA. http://ipcsav.org.s3.amazonaws.com/uploaded/w/0e420289_worship-and-music-today.pdf.

Jones, Paul S. *Singing and Making Music: Issues in Church Music Today.* Philadelphia: P&R, 2006.

Kauflin, Bob. *Worship Matters: Leading Others to Encounter the Greatness of God.* Wheaton, IL: Crossway, 2008.

Kilde, Jeanne Halgren. *When Church Became Theatre: The Transformation of Evangelical Architecture and Worship in Nineteenth-Century America.* New York: Oxford University Press, 2002.

Koester, Craig R. "The Distant Triumph Song: Music and the Book of Revelation." *Word and World* 12/3 (1992) 243–62.

Lane, Deforia. *Music as Medicine.* Chicago: Zondervan, 1996.

Lewis, Clive Staples. *Mere Christianity.* San Francisco: Harper, 2001.

———. "On Church Music." In *Christian Reflections*, 94–99. Grand Rapids: Eerdmans, 1967.

Lull, Timothy F., and William R. Russell. *Martin Luther's Basic Theological Teachings.* Minneapolis: Fortress, 2012.

Madsen, Grant R. "The Science of Singing." *BYU Magazine* (Spring 2002) n.p. http://magazine.byu.edu/?act=view&a=981.

Man, Ron. *Proclamation and Praise: Hebrews 2:12 and the Christology of Worship.* Eugene, OR: Wipf & Stock, 2007.

Meyers, Jeffrey. *The Lord's Service: The Grace of Covenant Renewal Worship.* Moscow, ID: Canon, 2011.

Nelson, Seth N. "John Calvin's Theology of Music: An Introduction." *Covenant OPC Newsletter*, March 2011.

Old, Hughes O. *Worship: Reformed According to Scripture.* Louisville: Westminster John Knox, 2002.

Parker, Alice. *Melodious Accord: Good Singing in Church.* Chicago: GIA, 1991.

Peterson, David. *Engaging with God: A Biblical Theology of Worship.* Downers Grove, IL: InterVarsity, 2002.

Piper, John. *Brothers, We Are Not Professionals: A Plea to Pastors for Radical Ministry.* Nashville: B & H, 2002.

————. *Desiring God: Meditations of a Christian Hedonist.* Colorado Springs: Waterbrook Multnomah, 2003.

Polanyi, Michael. *Personal Knowledge.* Chicago: University of Chicago Press, 1962.

Pruitt, Todd. "Is Your Church Worship More Pagan Than Christian?" http://www.christianity.com/church/worship-and-hymns/is-your-church-worship-more-pagan-than-christian.html.

————. "Is Your Worship Christian or Pagan? (7 Tests)." http://www.christianity.com/church/worship-and-hymns/is-your-worship-christian-or-pagan-7-tests.html.

Ross, Allen P. *Recalling the Hope of Glory.* Grand Rapids: Kregel Academic, 2006.

Routley, Eric. *Twentieth Century Church Music.* Carol Stream, IL: Agape, 1964.

Sayers, Dorothy L. *The Mind of the Maker.* London: Muethen, 1941.

Siemon-Netto, Uwe. "Why Nippon Is Nuts about J. S. Bach." *The Atlantic Times*, December 2005. http://www.atlantic-times.com/archive_detail.php?recordID=386.

Sproul, R.C. "Denying God's Transcendence." http://www.ligonier.org/learn/devotionals/denying-gods-transcendence/.

Spurgeon, Charles Haddon. "Heavenly Worship." Sermon No. 110. http://www.spurgeon.org/sermons/0110.htm.

Stetzer, Ed, and Elmer Towns. *Perimeters of Light.* Chicago: Moody, 2004.

Strobel, Lee. *Inside the Mind of Unchurched Harry and Sally.* Chicago: Zondervan, 1993.

Swan, Frederic. "The President's Report." *The American Organist* (February 2011) 2–3.

Thomas, André J. *Way Over in Beulah Lan': Understanding and Performing the Negro Spiritual.* Dayton, OH: Heritage Music, 2007.

Toledo, David, M. "Created in God's Image: Humanity's Doxological Vision." http://www.davidmtoledo.com/wp-content/uploads/2014/06/Created-in-Gods-Image-Toledo.pdf.

Tommasini, Anthony. "The Greatest." *New York Times*, January 21, 2011. http://www.nytimes.com/2011/01/23/arts/music/23composers.html?pagewanted=all&_r=0.

Tozer, A. W. *The Incredible Christian: How Heaven's Children Live on Earth.* Camp Hill, PA: Wing Spread, 2010.

————. *The Pursuit of God.* Atlanta: Stori, 2013.

————. *The Root of the Righteous.* Harrisburg, PA: Christian Publications, 1955.

————. *The Size of the Soul.* Camp Hill, PA: Wing Spread, 2010.

————. *Tozer on Worship and Entertainment.* Edited by James L. Snyder. Chicago: Wingspread, 2006.

————. *Whatever Happened to Worship?* Camp Hill, PA: Wing Spread, 2006.

Troeger, Thomas H. *Music as Prayer: The Theology and Practice of Church Music.* Oxford: Oxford University Press, 2013.

Twain, Mark. *Letters from the Earth.* Edited by Bernard DeVoto. Greenwich, CT: Fawcett Crest, 1962.

BIBLIOGRAPHY

Wainright, Geoffrey, and Karen B. Westerfield Tucker. *The Oxford History of Christian Worship*. Oxford: Oxford University Press, 2006.

Ware, Timothy (Kallistos). "The Earthly Heaven." In *Eastern Orthodox Theology: A Contemporary Reader*, edited by Daniel Clendenin, 11–20. Grand Rapids: Baker, 1995.

Warfield, B. B. *Calvin as a Theologian and Calvinism Today*. Philadelphia: Presbyterian Board of Education, 1909.

Webber, Robert E. *Worship Old and New*. Rev. ed. Chicago: Zondervan, 2009.

Westermann, Claus. *Blessing in the Bible and the Life of the Church*. Minneapolis: Fortress, 1978.

———. *Praise and Lament in the Psalms*. Translated by K. R. Crim and R. N. Soulen. Atlanta: John Knox, 1981.

Wilson, Monte E. "Church-O-Rama or Corporate Worship." In *The Compromised Church: The Present Evangelical Crisis*, edited by John H. Armstrong, 134–42. Wheaton, IL: Crossway, 1998.

Wilson-Dickson, Andrew. *The Story of Christian Music*. Minneapolis: Fortress, 1996.

Wren, Brian. *Praying Twice: The Music and Words of Congregational Song*. Louisville: Westminster John Knox, 2000.

Wuthnow, Robert. *After the Baby Boomers: How Twenty- and Thirty-Somethings Are Shaping the Future of American Religion*. Princeton, NJ: Princeton University Press, 2010.

Young, Carlton R. *Music of the Heart: John and Charles Wesley on Music and Musicians*. Carol Stream, IL: Hope, 1995.